CULTURAL GAPS

Endorsements

In the last two centuries, probably a million missionary years have been spent bringing the good news of the fathomless riches of Christ to Hindus in the great land of India. But whole libraries have been filled trying to answer the question, "Why has so little resulted from this magnificent effort?" Now, at last, this book is back in print. Happily, a new generation of readers will meet this most amazing, disturbing, admirable missionary of a hundred years ago, Benjamin Robinson.

Robinson aspired to live as close as possible to the Hindu ideal of a godly man, that he might win some. Most of the missionaries thought Robinson had gone too far; H. L. Richard, in the introduction, suggests that Robinson did not go far enough. Or, rather, Robinson "did not have enough time to properly develop, in the field now called contextual theology," his radical model through which the kingdom, the power, and the glory of God might be expressed in vast India. At last, this book is back in print. Christians in every cross-cultural context will gain greatly from it.

BOB BLINCOE
president of US Frontiers

H. L. Richard has done a great service in placing Benjamin Robinson's treasure in my hands to review. I warn the reader that a serious and sympathetic reading of Robinson himself (and of Richard's comments along the way) will be a spiritually disruptive experience and may not feel like a "service" as much as a stab to the heart. In the late nineteenth century Robinson landed in what he referred to as his new God-given land, full of expectation, and in many ways, a man of his times. But something happened that resulted in Robinson later being able to commend a man who referred to himself as a "Wesleyan Hindu." The story of that journey is not a story of contextualization as much as it is a story of a spiritual journey. Some may guess that this journey is from evangelical Christianity to some sort of pluralism, but in fact it is a spiritual journey into a deeper life in and for Christ. The journey was, to put it lightly, challenging: physically, spiritually, relationally, psychologically, and emotionally. His journey is not for everyone, and some readers may recoil. But for others, myself included, Robinson, in H. L Richard's explanatory presentation, invites us to join him, or better, to join Jesus on the path. In Robinson's own words, this is an invitation to discover, "The Lord's own method, life touching life to divine issues, began to grow plain; I was impelled to try to follow Him in that."

KEVIN HIGGINS
president, William Carey International University

This is a story that could be made into a movie. The final conclusion of this riveting saga is: The only meaningful way to reach Hindus is within their culture, specifically within their bhakti tradition. The only communicator they will respectfully listen to is one of Christ-like character.

HERBERT E. HOEFER
author of *Churchless Christianity*

Intercultural adventurers often remain hidden in obscurity across the historical landscape of divine-human interaction. The Israeli slave girl in Naaman the Syrian's household (2 Kgs 5:3) and those scattered disciples in Antioch from Cyprus and Cyrene (Acts 11:19–20) are among such figures tantalizingly mentioned in the Bible. Benjamin Robinson ventured from modern Britain into Indian Hindu communities, leaving behind an instructive legacy of intercultural witness, brokenness, and self-discovery. As part of his own adventure within Hindu realities, H. L. Richard has cast fresh light on Robinson's creative missionary witness and experimental interaction with the divine. All who similarly follow and serve Christ can learn much here.

J. NELSON JENNINGS
mission pastor, consultant, and international liaison, Onnuri Community Church, Seoul, South Korea

When I first heard my friend H. L. Richard use this small book to present the life and work of Benjamin Robinson, I heard a voice in my mind say, "He understands." Robinson understood several things that have characterized my life as a witness to the resurrection of Christ while living among Hindu communities. He understood them much better than I do because he risked experiencing them in a manner and at a level of intensity that far surpasses mine. He understood the polite rejection, isolated loneliness, and temptations to bitterness associated with his passionate life being reduced to little more than a cautionary tale. But he also discovered that the missions mainstream didn't even know all of the questions, let alone the answers, about the gospel thriving, or failing to thrive, among Hindu communities and within Hindu people. This did not console Robinson; it simply added a greater urgency to his faithfully attempting to do the impossible. It also increased the pain of what seemed to be his inability to fully complete his task. I am drawn to this moving story because I have taken one tiny sip of the cup Robinson drank. I deeply respect him.

TIMOTHY SHULTZ
author of *Disciple Making among Hindus*

Cultural Gaps *is a unique and stimulating account of one man's honest and courageous struggle to understand and engage men and women of another faith tradition. Benjamin Robinson's quest to understand Indians and their religious ways, his humility, and his service unto death offer modern Christian witnesses vital insights and cautions. More than a century after his death, Robinson still speaks and challenges us.*

MICHAEL W. STROOPE
M. C. Shook Chair of Missions, George W. Truett Theological Seminary

CULTURAL GAPS

Benjamin Robinson's Experience with Hindu Traditions

Edited by **H. L. RICHARD**
Foreword by **ART MCPHEE**

WILLIAM CAREY PUBLISHING

Cultural Gaps: Benjamin Robinson's Experience with Hindu Traditions
© 2020 by Frontier Ventures

All rights reserved.

Original text by Benjamin Robinson (1912)
Original Foreword by Henry Haigh (1912)
First edition published, London: Charles H. Kelly (1912)
Introduction, Notes, and Afterword by H. L. Richard
Foreword by Art McPhee
Front cover photo: Benjamin Robinson (1852–1913), Methodist Missionary Society archives at the School of Oriental and African Studies, London, file MMS/09/20/01 (MMS, India, Photographs, Box 1198).

No part of this book may be reproduced, stored in a retrieval system, or transmitted in any form or by any means—electronic, mechanical, photocopy, recording, or otherwise—without prior written permission of the publisher, except brief quotations used in connection with reviews in magazines or newspapers. For permission, email permissions@wclbooks.com.

Published by William Carey Publishing
10 W. Dry Creek Cir
Littleton, CO 80120 | www.missionbooks.org

William Carey Publishing is a ministry of Frontier Ventures
Pasadena, CA 91104 | www.frontierventures.org

Mike Riester, cover and interior design
Andy Sloan, copyeditor
Melissa Hicks, managing editor

ISBNs: 978-1-64508-188-3 (paperback),
　　　　978-1-64508-190-6 (mobi),
　　　　978-1-64508-191-3 (epub)

Printed Worldwide

24 23 22 21 20　　1 2 3 4 5

Library of Congress data on file with publisher

Contents

Map	ix
Foreword by Art McPhee	xi
Acknowledgments	xv
Introduction by H. L. Richard	xvii
Foreword to the First Edition by Henry Haigh	xxxiii
1. The Beginning of Understanding and Conviction	1
2. Experiences in Contextual Evangelism	11
3. Reflecting on Failure	23
4. Learning	33
5. Dialog with Brāhmans	45
6. Final Years of Brokenness	55
Afterword by H. L. Richard	61
Appendix 1: Reviews of the First Edition of This Book	65
Appendix 2: Benjamin Robinson's Engagement and Marriage	69
Appendix 3: The Missionary Lifestyle Debate in *The Harvest Field*	75
References	85
Index	89

Benjamin Robinson (1852-1913)
Source: Methodist Missionary Society archives at the School of Oriental and African Studies, London, file MMS/09/20/01 (MMS, India, Photographs, Box 1198)

"It is not easy to state accurately the mental processes of one's inner life.
Careful analysis will serve to a certain point, but beyond that
are thoughts and emotions which cannot be reduced to words.
This seems to be especially the case
with the first two years of a minister's life in India.
I can look back upon those mental changes and as it were live them over again,
but I fear it will be impossible to represent them fairly in words."

—Benjamin Robinson in "Memories II," *The Harvest Field*,
second series, vol. 6 no. 2, August 1885, page 43.

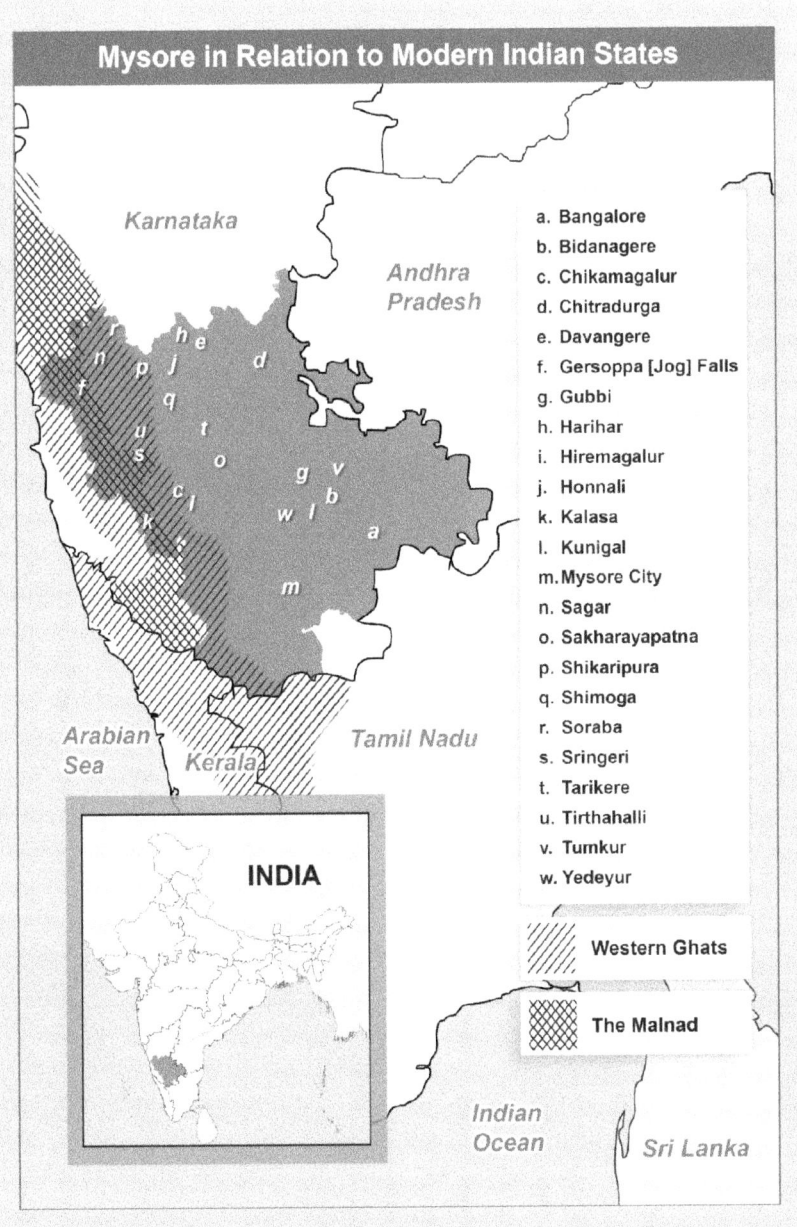

Foreword

In my library is a first edition of *In the Brāhmans' Holy Land: A Record of Service in the Mysore*, by Benjamin Robinson. Inside the cover is a presentation bookplate that says, "First Prize presented to Annie McLean for attendance and merit by Ebenezer Hall." The date is "22nd Dec. 1914," two years after the book's publication.

> When I saw the presentation plate, I imagined—because of the nature of the award, as well as the familiar form of the recipient's name—that Annie was, perhaps, still quite young. But why would a church group charged with giving a young person's award choose *that* book—a book about "a long martyrdom," as one historian described Robinson's missionary life? Why give perfect-attendee Annie McLean the memoir of a contrarian, whose against-the-grain approach to missions had been unappreciated by Indians he hoped to reach, doubted by colleagues with whom he worked, reproved by clerics who deemed him theologically edgy, and patronized by reviewers who labeled him naive?
>
> The answer comes easily to readers of the memoir who share Robinson's humble awe of the rigors and risks of sharing the gospel in an inscrutable alien culture. But it comes drudgingly, if not grudgingly, to readers comfortably tethered to their own alien cultures. I like to think that the Ebenezer Hall awarders who honored Annie McLean's attendance and merit were some of the former. So was John Owen Farquhar Murray, master of Selwyn College, Cambridge, when the book came out. He was one of the first reviewers.
>
> The importance of this book is not to be measured by its size. It is the record of a costly experiment made humbly and with whole-hearted self-surrender, and so, even when it seemed to fail, establishing conclusions of far-reaching significance.[1]

---

1. See appendix 1 for the full text of Murray's review.

The Reverend Benjamin Robinson was as serious, single-minded, and surrendered as Murray's statement affirmed. In 1882, when he was thirty, he sailed away to what he called his new "God-chosen home" in southern India. In what is now Karnataka, he served as an evangelist and catechist among the Kannadigas. As with all he did, he gave himself to the work wholly. It did not take him long, though, to realize his initial aim of learning the language, life, and worldview of people was not enough. For example, he learned that his leather Bible and appetite for meat were definite impediments. Indeed, he discovered he could offend Kannadiga sensibilities in many ways. So, he radicalized his program. He ate only what they ate. He studied their sacred texts. He adopted their dress and went barefoot. He scrupulously avoided anything unclean, polluted, or taboo. But the task he'd set for himself was more formidable a burden than he'd imagined. It wore him down mentally, psychologically, and physically. Seven years later, in 1889, he was compelled to return home, a broken man.

For three years, Robinson languished in pain that "knew no ease" and in misery that was "too dark for despair." And although he convalesced, his health remained tenuous. In 1912, Robinson published *In the Brāhmans' Holy Land: A Record of Service in the Mysore*. He wrote it during a final illness that foreshadowed his death in 1913.

Now I find that my friend, H. L. Richard, has dusted off Robinson's memoir—for the benefit of many, I hope—and, with fresh information and commentary added, is readying a new edition. He has not done so, of course, to spotlight Robinson's remarkable austerity program as a forgotten model for emulation—far from it—but, instead, as an example of the seriousness of purpose the gospel demands of all Christ-followers, and more, to bring to mind the unintended by-products of Robinson's rash pursuit: (1) his many perceptive glimpses into the Hindu world; and (2) lessons learned on the limits of missionary endeavors. Both are as useful to know today as in his day.

And there is yet another theme. H. L. Richard has long reminded the readers of his articles and books that the cultural chasms between East and West, and North and South, are too vast for dependence on a supra-cultural expression of the gospel. There is, in fact, no such thing as a supra-cultural gospel. As Robinson realized, the gospel of Jesus Christ, though universally true and applicable, must be uniquely expressed and lived in every cultural setting and generation. But to bring that about is a task to which no human is equal. Only Christ acting in and through his followers is equal to it.

Robinson highlights this idea in several passages, including this one:

> Caste is birth. Whatever you do, you cannot alter it. However you dress or eat, you will be and will be known as an Englishman. Your motives in change of dress would be misunderstood and misconstrued.... I could not, however much I wished, bridge over the chasms of birth, but all the more deeply was the need of spiritual re-birth pressed into me. The Lord's own method, life touching life to divine issues, began to grow plain; I was impelled to try to follow Him in that. (pg. 25)

H. L. Richard has, in previous books, helped us—through the lives and thoughts of eminent Indian interpreters of the gospel—like the Marathi poet, Narayan Vaman Tilak, and the Bengali evangelist, R. C. Das, and K. Subba Rao of Andhra—to see the folly of an evangelism that is not contextual and is not carried out under the superintendence and in the power of the Spirit. In accord with those who selected Robinson's little volume to present to Annie McLean, he now points us to an Englishman, alongside Tilak and Das and Subba Rao, as one ready to remind us too.

—Art McPhee
professor emeritus (Sundo Kim Chair of Evangelism and Practical Theology)
Asbury Theological Seminary
September 14, 2019

Acknowledgments

I have been using the excellent library and archives at the United Theological College (UTC) in Bangalore off and on for over twenty-five years, and again I am indebted to the staff there for assistance in this project. The archives of the Wesleyan Methodist Missionary Society at the School of Oriental and African Studies (SOAS) in London contained a great deal of useful information, and the knowledgeable and helpful staff there are acknowledged with gratitude.

I first gained access to Benjamin Robinson's text through the marvelous system of interlibrary loan in the United States. A decade after the fact, I do not even remember what library provided me in southern California with a microfilm copy of the 1912 edition published by Charles H. Kelly in London. I printed off each page of that microfilm, and my wife, without whom I cannot imagine having done what I have done in life, typed out an electronic version of that copy from microfilm. This expression of thanks for her work on this manuscript is an extreme understatement.

My friends at William Carey Publishing proposed a new title for this new edition of Benjamin Robinson's reflections on his engagement with Hindus. My thanks to them for this and many other assistances.

It has long been my habit to seek help, suggestions, corrections, improvements, etc., from a wide range of friends and co-workers for all of my writings. This reprint of Benjamin Robinson's stirring record was stimulated by encouraging responses received from a review of this book that I wrote and privately circulated in 2008. The afterword and chapter subheadings were prepared after specific suggestions from two of these friends, and many other details of the text were prepared, corrected, or improved thanks to others. Special thanks must be rendered to Art McPhee for his insightful foreword.

Robinson dedicated the first edition of this book "to all who love mankind." I dedicate this edition to my helpful friends who share Robinson's and my concern for the way of Christ in the Hindu world.

Introduction by H. L. Richard

The book in your hands, first published over a century ago, is a rare treasure. I have been unable to forget it since reading a microfilmed copy over a decade ago. Lessons here for twenty-first century Christianity are abundant and profound, and particularly in the area of ministry among Hindus this is an essential read. Well over a century after Benjamin Robinson struggled in south India, witnesses for Christ among Hindus today still grapple with many of the same issues he faced. For modern *sādhaks* (practitioners of a spiritual path), reading Robinson will be good for the soul.

Seeds toward understanding the failure of Christianity in Asia are also in this book. On the fringes of the great Asian civilizational/religious traditions, and on the ruins of the destructive Cultural Revolution in China, Christianity has taken root; but Christianity primarily remains alien to Asian traditions. In India, few have wrestled deeply with Hindu traditions and what good news means in that complex world, again with an exception for the fringes where ttribal and Dalit peoples have embraced Christianity.[2] Benjamin Robinson is a unique figure in Protestant missions to India, and there are three reasons to listen to this account of his struggles and suffering (not merely physical suffering, although health problems brought a premature end to his time in India, and to his life).

Why Read Robinson Now?

First, Robinson looked in the eyes of his task and the impossibility of crossing the cultural gaps between himself and Hindus. His humility and desire to learn and understand are especially commendable. But it was his respect for the magnitude of the task of representing Christ to Hindus that most stands out. "Who is sufficient for these things?" asked the Apostle Paul (2 Cor 2:16),

---

2. Roger Hedlund stated this clearly in 1995: "Despite Christianity's success in India, however, its track record in evangelising the Hindu majority could best be described as massive neglect" (1995, 82).

and that must still be the attitude of any who would approach Hindus to speak of Jesus. It was after years of involvement in India that Robinson could state, "Then I began to learn a little of my ignorance" (pg. 29). The failure of Christianity in Asia is rooted in similar ignorance, and there is no hope for improvement without a deep commitment to humble learning.

Second, Robinson's text indicates the type of transformation that takes place in the life of a follower of Jesus who engages at a serious level with followers of other faith traditions. How true of many (one dares to suggest most) missionaries is his suggestion that "It seemed as if all the years of discipleship had but made Him say of me, 'You know not what manner of spirit you are of'" (pg. 28, referring to Christ's words in Luke 9:55 in the King James Version). Deep engagement with other faith traditions and cultures strips away the tidy comforts of Christian thought and culture. This leaves one facing what often seems like an abyss. But grappling with the meaning of Christ at this level, facing the realities of personal reliance on cultural traditions rather than on Christ, draws one to the deepest foundations of faith. This leads to perspectives that are truly wise, and more to be valued than gold or rubies (Prov 3:13–15, etc.)

Finally, this text is provocative for missiological thought related to lovers of Christ who refuse Christianity, or what Herb Hoefer called non-baptized believers in Christ. Where else does one read about a self-professed "Wesleyan Hindu" (pg. 25)? Clearly, Robinson and his co-workers had no paradigm for relating to such people; concepts like multiple religious belonging and insider movements had not yet arisen. So the "what ifs" of Robinson's study are compelling: What if Robinson had been a bit more cautious and did not shatter his health? What if the missionary movement as a whole had (or still yet might learn to have) as much respect for Hindu traditions and the task of sharing Christ with Hindus as Robinson demonstrated? What if those few Hindu lovers of Jesus had been encouraged to develop whole new patterns of discipleship to Jesus?

In India in the 1880s, when author Benjamin Robinson lived out the experiences outlined in this book, his missionary colleagues did not approve of his approach. When this account was first published in 1912, it cemented the response that this book and effort are misguided.[3] A century later we need

---

3. The review published in the *International Review of Missions* in 1913 shows this rejection of Robinson's approach. That review is in appendix 1 of this volume (pgs. 65-66). See also the information in note 11.

to revisit the story, as the record of failure for Christianity has continued for yet another century.[4]

Benjamin Robinson

Benjamin Robinson (1852–1913) was a missionary from England in the Wesleyan Methodist Missionary Society (WMMS) in the region of south India then called Mysore, now the state of Karnataka.[5] His official work was educational, but he was not satisfied with the running of institutions.[6] In the definitive history of the WMMS, authors G. G. Findlay and W. W. Holdsworth stated that

> the Rev. B. Robinson was one who, so far as human foresight can declare, would have attained to a position of immense influence, but unhappily his ministry was cut short by a complete breakdown of health.... (1924, 288)[7]

---

4. Robinson's book was reprinted around 1938 by The Epworth Press. In the wondrous world of twenty-first century book-buying, I am now the owner of a copy of this edition, purchased online from a bookseller in Australia. There is no date of publication in this edition, and no explanation for why the title was reprinted; it is an exact reproduction of the original, including the foreword by Henry Haigh.
It is odd that no copies of this edition are listed in the WorldCat library system.
The reprint prompted a review (more like a synopsis) by N. C. Sargent in the *National Christian Council Review* in 1939 (thus the guess of a publication date of 1938).
The title of Sargent's piece, "Indian Dress: The Story of a Costly Experiment," sufficiently indicates his perspective, which is in full agreement with the earlier narrative.
5. See the map on pg. ix. Robinson often mentions Mysore in his text, updated in this edition to Karnataka as the current name for most of that region. The Hoysala kingdom in the twelfth and thirteenth centuries began the modern history of the Mysore region. There were four Anglo-Mysore wars where the great Hyder Ali (1722-1782) and his son Tipu Sultan (1750-1799) challenged and were challenged by the growing power of the British, who finally took control in 1799 while still allowing Mysore the status of an independent kingdom. The map identifies all places mentioned by Robinson in his text (current spellings are used, and are indicated in square brackets in the text). Besides changing Robinson's title, I have also Americanized spellings, modernized punctuation (particularly eliminating numerous capitalizations that are unnecessary by today's standards), and made other changes to the text which are indicated in the notes.
6. The archives of the WMMS in Bangalore indicate that Robinson's appointment was to the "educational department" (UTC, Synod Minutes 1877-1897, C37/B, MMS 21, 212 [1882], 259 [1884]). This educational focus is also clear from Robinson's text where he states that "my whole self was given in hardest work to the normal students" (pg. 52). A "normal school," according to the Encyclopedia Britannica, is an "institution for the training of teachers" (https://www.britannica.com/topic/normal-school). Robinson's role as an educator is also clear in the history of the WMMS:
> ... in 1883 a normal school was begun in Shimoga. Later on, under the management of the Rev. B. Robinson, this attained a high degree of efficiency, and from the point of view of this branch of work alone the breakdown in the health of that most devoted missionary was a great loss to the district. (Findlay and Holdsworth 1924, 287)
7. A similar statement appears from Robinson's co-workers in Karnataka, who wrote expressing regret at his early departure due to illness:
> Mr. Robinson devoted himself from the beginning with rare patience and determination to the study of Kanarese and Sanskrit and at the time of

That complete breakdown of health seems to have been directly related to the radical approach to cultural adaptation (indigenization was the term at that time, contextualization is today's term) that Robinson embraced. His record is deeply moving, as he wrestles with failure and then with his broken health, and is deeply instructive as he insists on learning and humbly adapting.

Robinson's Life

Benjamin Robinson was born on September 10, 1852, in Wellingborough in Northamptonshire, England. He trained for the Methodist ministry at Didsbury College in Manchester from 1877–80. After a year of service in the Methodist Church in England, he left for India in 1882. In an anonymous paper written in 1885, he reflected on his arrival in India and his long emotional relationship to that country:

> Soon I stood upon the shore of my God-chosen home. Wonderingly, as a child I had heard of it from the lips of those now dead, and had fancied it in childish dreams. When study had become the intense passion of my life at college, it was written on my heart and was present to my thought day and night. I saw it with emotion I cannot name and prayed that I might become a minister of Jesus Christ according to God's will. (Robinson 1885a, 10)[8]

Robinson left behind in England a young woman to whom he was betrothed, and the eventual breaking off of that relationship in 1888 is a dramatic backstory to this text (see appendix 2 for details). Robinson was married for less than a year of his time in India. His wife helped nurse him through four inactive years after his return from India in 1889, and also during his final two inactive years when he wrote this book. From 1893 to 1910 Robinson was active in the Methodist ministry in Scotland and England, being remembered

---

his collapse was well on his way to a profound acquaintance with those languages. We had hoped that in due time this country might receive from his pen useful contributions to biblical & theological literature; and indeed we still hope, though your letter suggests very serious apprehension. We pray for Bro Robinson that he may receive comfort & enlargement in this discipline, and that sooner than seems at present likely, he may, in the goodness of God be permitted to return. (UTC, "Reply to the Committee's Letter," Bangalore, January 1890, in "Minutes of Mysore District Meeting Bangalore Jan 2nd 1890," in Synod Minutes 1877-1897 C37/B MMS 21, 442; the letter is signed by J. Hudson, chairman, and G. H. Hocken, secretary)

8. The three-part anonymous article on "Memories" published in *The Harvest Field* in 1885 is certainly by Benjamin Robinson. The general style and contents support this, with definitive evidence lying in the third part, where an incident is related that also appears in this book; see the story on remembering deeds from childhood and the scripture itself as proof (1885c, 83; in this book pgs. 29-30). *The Harvest Field* was published by Robinson's Methodist co-workers in south India.

as "an exemplary pastor" and "a great teacher" (Wesleyan Methodist Church 1913, 132).[9] He died on March 20, 1913.

Interpreting Benjamin Robinson

Robinson's work, and his record of it in this book, was interpreted in the light of controversies in the mission world of his time. Simmering issues in British Methodism related to missionary lifestyles broke out publicly just as Robinson was leaving India.[10] The Salvation Army had arrived in India in 1882 with their radical approach to adaptation, which included going without shoes. Just months before Robinson's first experiment (described in chapter 2) in 1885 there was a meeting in Bangalore on "Asceticism in the Indian Church," which was reported in the March 1885 edition of *The Harvest Field*. The report concluded by saying,

> It was felt that while we honour the spirit which leads a man to give up European food, clothing, and manner of life, we cannot but regard such procedure as a distinct misrepresentation of Christianity, and as an unhappy homage to the ascetic spirit of Hinduism. (*Wesleyan Methodist News* 1885, 283)

This provides context for the hesitations that Robinson describes in chapter 1. It also helps explain how Benjamin Robinson became a test case in the argument against adopting an Indian standard of living. Findlay and Holdsworth refer to him as "a martyr to the attempt so complacently proposed on paper" (1921, 159), living at local standards being the proposal. Robinson's own critique of this lifestyle is presented (unacknowledged) by

---

9. The biographical details in these paragraphs are from this 1913 obituary. There are details about the places Robinson ministered from 1893 to 1910 in Methodist Publishing House 1912, 201. The picture of Robinson which appears on pg. viii is clearly from these later years in the UK, and can be found in the SOAS archives at MMS/09/20/01, portraits of mission personnel and church members.
10. The Methodist controversy is explained in detail in Findlay and Holdsworth's history of the WMMS. In summary, the *Methodist Times* in 1889 suggested that missionaries in India were living a high life, out of touch with the common people. This was especially in light of the mission policy of running schools to educate higher caste Hindu children (Robinson's assigned task). The charge was refuted, those who originally made the charges recanted, and there was healthy reconciliation (Findlay and Holdsworth 1921, 136-160). The entire issue of the June 1889 *The Harvest Field* magazine was devoted to defending the missionaries from the charges against them

Findlay and Holdsworth.[11] In so far as Robinson was remembered, it was as a warning against attempting such a lifestyle.[12]

But this was just one aspect of Robinson's quest, and arguably the least important. By two-thirds of the way through chapter 3, Robinson had concluded that he would not dress like an Indian, yet his struggle to communicate was still barely beginning. ("Those convictions made one outward method of work impossible to me, but the purpose and aim of that method, the aim of my life, was still beyond," pg. 28.) Note also the full repudiation of Indian dress in his 1889 article: "Ultimately I felt it was my duty to abandon Hindu dress" (Robinson 1889b, 45).

Robinson's Insights

Robinson's record of his service from 1882–89 begins where he began as a missionary, with a lesson on language and culture. It is a strange poem and story that opens the book. Don't toss the book aside; Robinson wants you to *feel* what he experienced, which is *the fundamental lack of resonance between Western Christianity and Hindu traditions.* That lesson is driven home in succeeding chapters, until the story of Robinson's broken health takes over.

---

11. Findlay and Holdsworth wrote, "On the principles of Hinduism, birth fixes immovable barriers between race and race, caste and caste, and for the stranger to affect Hindu customs in dress, diet, and the like, is an intrusion which he resents as a kind of sacrilege" (1921, 158). See Robinson's discussion on these lines on pg. pgs. 24-28, and see also my discussion below on problematic aspects of this analysis. By 1889 Robinson had definitively rejected dressing in the local style, but he never so strongly rejected either the principle of adaptation or the helpfulness of an adjusted diet.

12. Robinson and his book first came to my attention through the following comments by William Emilsen.
    > By the beginning of the twentieth century, Protestant attitudes to missionary identification had changed very little. While the heroic nature of various attempts were applauded, missionary administrators generally regarded them as misguided, costly to health, doomed to failure, and ultimately offensive to Indian as well as European sensibilities. The experiences of the Wesleyan Methodist missionary of Mysore, Benjamin Robinson, who died in 1913, were often cited as proof. Robinson was sent in 1882 to the Mysore district where he worked for seven years before he was taken back to England with his health shattered. Like de Nobili before him, Robinson had felt himself called to live as the Indian in an attempt to remove any barriers which separated him from those among whom he came to labour, and he published a record of his experiences, *In the Brāhmans' Holy Land*, shortly before his death. Assessments of his experiment were overwhelmingly negative. His had been a costly experiment, which invariably placed the missionary on a slippery slope to a pointless martyrdom. It should never be repeated:
    >> ... in its eager purpose that the messenger might become an Indian to the Indians it failed entirely.... The lesson of that first and most extreme form of the experiment was only that caste is jati, "birth," and between Englishmen and Hindu there is a great gulf fixed which even love and sacrifice cannot bridge. (J. H. Moulton in *Religions and Religion: A Study of the Science of Religion, Pure and Applied*, The Forty-third Fernley Lecture. London: Charles H Kelly, 1913, 168.) (Emilsen 1994, 42-43)

Introduction by H. L. Richard

This is a threatening subject. If Western Christianity does not resonate with Hindu traditions, if the gospel as we understand it is fundamentally foreign in the Indic world, the missionary effort is not only in vain but is a completely misguided venture. Benjamin Robinson saw this, and grappled with the implications.[13] This was and is not a new idea; note Robinson's reference to the Roman Catholic missionary Dubois who stated that no Hindu would ever convert to Christianity (pg. 9). Many, even among sincere Christians, have given up on the traditional mission enterprise, embracing pluralistic theologies that affirm that all religions are somehow in the end the same.

Western Christianity in a Global World

Robinson does not walk on these paths. But he is insistent that we feel this massive cultural gap—how inappropriate traditional Christianity is in Hindu contexts. Robinson asks, "How far does my life defile Christ's message?" (pg. 8). He does not refer to the honest failings of a follower of Christ, but rather to *perceived* defilement related to the cultural differences between Christian and Hindu traditions. Robin Boyd many years later appropriately referred to "the Latin captivity of the church" (1974), but Boyd was mainly dealing with theology, and his analysis does not provide the impact of Robinson's account. This should be the first lesson in missionary training; how alien both we and our message are, and how much we need to listen and learn.

Of course, missiology has developed a tidy little response: that the gospel will always be foreign in all contexts, including even the "Christian" West. This is true, but it is also a very different reality than the foreignness of Western Christianity in Hindu contexts. If the former truth masks the latter, it is worse than a lie. Robinson knew what he was experiencing, and he knew that Western Christianity had to die if the gospel was to take root in Hindu contexts. True, Robinson never used these exact words; he did write about "the reconsideration of all our own schemes and systems" (pg. 42), and I am certain he meant that fully literally.

---

13. The implication some drew, such as J. O. F. Murray of Cambridge (see his comments in his review of Robinson's book in appendix 1), was that Hinduism must be destroyed. That also seems to be the implication of the statement by J. H. Moulton quoted in the preceding note. Robinson certainly does not go in this direction.

On this point Robinson's humility again shines through, as he wrote in 1885:

> We are so apt to confound our poverty-stricken conception of the truth with the boundless wealth of the truth itself. To avoid this is no easy task. I know that we believe we have the Heavenly Form of the Truth Incarnate Himself before us. But who would dare to say that as he tries to present that Truth to others, his own conceptions may not dim that Glory? The almost overwhelming fear recoils upon me every time I try to preach, lest my presentation of that Perfect Loveliness should have marred it in the eyes of men. Rather than be in danger of thinking my conception of that Glory is as it should be, I would look forward into the unseen, revealing future, remembering the almost dying words of the profound and saintly Owen, "The long-wished-for day is come at last, in which I shall see *that glory* in another manner than I have ever done, or was capable of doing, in this world." (1885c, 78, quoting *Works of John Owen* vol. 1, ciii; italics added by Robinson)

Robinson's Quest Cut Short

Yet Robinson's insights about reconsidering theological systems remained strangely undeveloped. As the deep Western Christian that he was, Robinson's piety and his evangelism focused on personal sin, and on Christ as sin-bearer. These are no doubt biblical concepts, yet they did not resonate with his Hindu friends. This pushed Robinson to an even deeper focus on sin, and to a search of Hindu traditions to find support for his perspective. At what point, had he been able to continue his work, might he have noticed that devotion to the person of Christ (which was clearly developing in some of his friends) is more central to biblical thought even than personal sin? How might he have changed his emphasis, and begun reconsidering Western Christian "schemes and systems"?

Robinson does not indicate that he ever made approaches to what today would be called "contextual theology," but the reason for this is not far below the surface of his narrative. Robinson was deeply moved by the glaring disconnect between his understanding of society and the realities of caste-based Indian society. In the late nineteenth century there were still cases of death ceremonies for high-caste converts to Christianity, as shown in one of Robinson's moving portraits of his Hindu friends. Christianity was perceived by Hindus, and it was a largely accurate perception, as an alternative civilization. Missiological thought now repudiates this concept, and listens with empathy to the kinds of stories that Robinson tells in anticipation of better patterns and paradigms.

Fulfillment Theology

The great mission exploration of the decades around Robinson's time of service in India related to fulfillment theology, and there is certainly resonance between that approach and Robinson. Fulfillment theology recognized that the Christianity that had been presented to India was inadequate; it was triumphalistic and it denigrated other faith traditions in its certainties. Fulfillment theology proposed that there is much good in all religious traditions, and these good ideas and practices point toward Jesus Christ, who is the fulfillment of the best of human thought and endeavor.

In the classic statement of fulfillment theology, J. N. Farquhar's *The Crown of Hinduism*, Farquhar suggested that "Hinduism must die in order to live. It must die into Christianity" (1915, 51). This was first published just a year after Robinson's record, and I suggest that Farquhar is radically in error while Robinson has hit the mark. It is not that "Hinduism" (Farquhar's simplistic use of that term, not unrelated to Robinson's perspective, has been exposed in the scholarship of the last century; see below) must die, but that Western Christianity must die.[14] Again, Robinson never says this in such blunt terms, but it seems to me the clear lesson of his record; it also accounts for why the missionary movement did not pay any heed to his message, which was simply too threatening to "business as usual."

Of course, much has changed in India since the 1880s. Some of what at that time seemed to be "established truths" have been debunked; some even seem rather laughable now. Two such issues hold major importance to Robinson's study, so "caste" and "Hinduism" will be brought into focus.

Robinson on Caste

At the present time, there is still no academic consensus on how to evaluate caste. The history of caste is highly disputed. Its essence, if there is one, is contested; the diversity of its manifestations is profound and perplexing. As one of the better analysts of caste, Declan Quigley, noted, "The conventional portrayal of caste, as one might find it in a standard textbook of sociology, or, one should add, as one might find it in the accounts of many Hindus themselves, is riddled with problems" (1994, 28). Robinson shared what Quigley called the conventional perspective that was developed by Orientalist scholars seeking to identify the essence of Indian and Hindu traditions.

---

14. Western Christianity must die in Asian contexts, not necessarily in its own contexts.

Ronald Inden particularly laments this misreading of India, and his analysis is highly recommended (1990, 49–84).

Robinson's anecdotes of encounters with caste are fascinating, mostly due to the *contrast* with current caste practices.[15] Modernity has had a massive impact on India, and pollution from contact with people of other castes is nowhere near as dominant as an idea or practice today as it was in Robinson's time, if indeed Robinson is not also reading more into his encounters than he should have. Caste remains an issue of great importance (and controversy) in Hindu contexts, but in ways quite different and much more subtle than in Robinson's time.[16] Robinson's reference to "the sectional antagonisms of castes, which would make the universal purpose of God's love in Christ for all men as brothers impossible" (pg. 28) needs critique. No human society has come close to total egalitarianism; certainly not Victorian Britain, which one could argue also made "the universal purpose of God's love in Christ for all men as brothers impossible."

Robinson on "Hinduism"

It is interesting that "Hinduism" is never mentioned in Robinson's text; but this reality overshadows everything. In an article written in 1885 Robinson insightfully referred to the "by no means decaying, myriad-formed systems of idolatry which by a crude generalization Englishmen call Hinduism" (1985b, 44). Yet Robinson shared an erroneous assumption about a unified essence of Hinduism. In a letter written in 1885, Robinson expressed "an almost irresistible passion to press into the complete knowledge of the key to Indian thinking" (SOAS Library, WMMS India Correspondence Mysore 1879–1895, box #34, microfiche #1486, letter from Robinson to Jenkins, August 21, 1885).

Similarly, Robinson published a series of anonymous articles in 1885 that again show a desire to grasp the essence of Hindu thought. In the same article quoted above about Hinduism as a "crude generalization" he stated that "knowledge of the exact position of Hindus and sympathy with them seemed absolutely

---

15. In his paper published under the pseudonym A. Vidyarthi, Robinson insightfully commented on "strong caste-feeling which seems to increase as one descends in the social scale" (Robinson 1885e, 142). The general style and contents of this paper clearly point to Robinson, and full confirmation that he is the author is present in the story of the man who in a disturbed tone told his son he must learn the Vedas from Robinson (Robinson 1885e, 143 and pg. 15 in this book).
16. The critics of Robinson quoted previously (notes 10 and 11) perpetuated his inadequate perspective on caste, reifying an unchangeable institution, which has in fact undergone quite astonishing changes in the past century to the point of completely nullifying those earlier perspectives.

essential" (1885b, 47). Similarly, in the following article, focused on karma in Indian thought, he affirmed that "I long to know the secret of its intense fascination especially to the Hindu mind, so that I may feel their position, not merely understand it" (1885c, 81). The desire for empathy and feeling what Hindus feel cannot be too highly commended, but the assumption that there is a single key to Hinduism, let alone to "Indian thinking," is one of the great errors of earlier generations of students of Hindu traditions.

Robinson carefully observed and learned about the particularities of various types of Hindus (and types of Brāhmans). Yet some glaring cases of misrepresentation are present, perhaps particularly the statement that "The Veda is the highest characteristic expression of the Hindu genius and spirit. It is their very own—the spirit and life of their blood" (pg. 43). No doubt Robinson was told this by some of his Brāhman friends, and he should not be despised for believing it; but it is a romantic and propagandistic statement rather than a statement of fact.[17]

In his study of missionary constructions of Hinduism in the nineteenth century (appropriately titled *Imagined Hinduism*), Geoffrey Oddie commented on the failure of missionaries to understand Hindu realities right up to the end of the century:

> Missionaries may have placed undue emphasis on pantheism partly because of their ignorance of *bhakti* (loving devotion to a personal god) or failure to see it as a distinctive tradition. There was, indeed, comparatively little discussion of *bhakti* among European scholars for the greater part of the nineteenth century and it was only in the 1880s and 1890s that Ramanuja's philosophy, "dualism" and the ideas implicit in *bhakti* movements appear to have received much systematic attention. (2006, 270)

In this light, it is interesting to note that Robinson's account discusses three major *bhakti* (devotional) movements, without any mention of devotion as a central concept! These three are the Shiva *bhakti* Lingāyats, whom Robinson refers to with the Brāhmanical tag of *heretics* (pg. 3, see notes there); the Mādhvas, still often noted for their dualist theology more than for the centrality of *bhakti* in their system; and the Srivaiṣṇavas, the major *sampradāya* (denomination or sect) coming down from the greatest of the *bhakti*

---

17. Note Klaus Klostermaier's dangerously absolute but much more accurate statement that "The Puranas, neglected and rejected by the rationalistic nineteenth century as representing a corruption of Vedic religion and childish fabulation, have regained, in Indological scholarship, too, the central place they have always occupied in living Hinduism" (1994, 94).

theologians, Ramanuja. Modern understanding demands an interpretive standpoint very different from Robinson's, but his account insightfully points in important directions and stimulates critically needed analysis.

Did Robinson Go Too Far?

I have suggested that Robinson did not go far enough, rather did not have enough time to properly develop, in the field now called contextual theology. At the same time, he clearly went too far in his attempts to live simply, on the level of the local people. This is not an outside opinion, but Robinson's own conclusion about his first barefooted journey during an Indian summer, written in 1889: "I could not shut my eyes to the fact that I had transgressed God's laws of health, and that six weeks' illness was a warning, as well as an indication as to true economy in God's service" (1889b, 45).

Yet, also in 1889, he wrote an appeal for support for educational missions that included this statement:

> I have done all I can; have lived as near starvation as I could to start these schools. I cannot starve my wife; but we do live in as cheap a fashion as possible (in such a way that I should be ashamed of were it not for God's work's sake), so that we may do all we can.... There are times when the thought of the vast work around me drives away sleep, and it seems as if the work keeps piling up upon one until my head and heart would give way were it not for God's grace and the tender care of my wife. Mrs. Robinson is at work at the language, sometimes I fear beyond her strength in this heat. ("Letter from Rev. B. Robinson," in "Letters—India," *Wesleyan Missionary Society Woman's Work as Conducted by the Ladies' Auxiliary Quarterly Paper* No. 121, July 1889, 178–81)

How much hyperbole is in this last statement is open to debate. It is ironic to find Robinson concerned about his wife overworking in the heat!

In the end, it is not possible to know for certain how much of Robinson's health breakdown was related to his intensity of concern and his commitment to a simple lifestyle. It is noteworthy that just two months after Robinson's forced departure from India another missionary, Walter Sackett, newer to the field than Robinson, was also forced to leave due to health problems (Wesleyan 1889, 192). That warnings related to Robinson's health breakdown became his lasting legacy to the missionary movement is tragic indeed. This publication hopes to begin righting the record in this regard.

Introduction by H. L. Richard

Henry Haigh

Along with reprinting Robinson's anguished account, the original foreword by Henry Haigh (1853–1917, in India from 1875 to 1901, a secretary of the WMMS in London from 1901 to 1917) is included. Haigh was a reputed missionary, referenced in Findlay and Holdsworth's history of the WMMS as

> a great idealist. His mind was quick in grasping large conceptions of missionary operations, and the enthusiasm with which he set to work to bring those conceptions to good effect was boundless. His schemes of work were often so far in advance of the actual present that they were sometimes received with hesitation and misgiving by his colleagues, but there was no gainsaying the fact that they were finely conceived, and on a large and generous scale. (1924, 291)

Consider Haigh's words about Robinson's book carefully; he understood that his friend Robinson was wrestling with the true issues. A few years after Robinson left India, Haigh spoke at the great Bombay decennial missionary gathering of 1892 words that resonate with Robinson's experience and perspective:

> The principle I contend for, then, is this: *that the books which we publish should be carefully related to Hindu thought, expressed in its terms, done in its style, adopting where it can its positions, and leading on, still in Hindu fashion and in its terminology, from points of agreement to essential points of difference.* In this way we may, perhaps, be able to furnish an effectual exhibition of legitimately "Hinduized Christianity." (Haigh 1893, 667; italics original)

Haigh's dream was never realized, and Robinson's effort in a similar direction came to naught. But traditional Christianity has not proven persuasive, and modern insights into culture and religion suggest that Robinson and Haigh were probing in the right direction. With a far more nuanced understanding of Hindu traditions, and living with a caste system that has been radically transformed from their times, careful listening to Benjamin Robinson will provoke stimulating insights and responses.

About This Edition

A few other points should be made about this text. Before he left India in 1889, Robinson wrote two articles for *The Harvest Field* which anticipate this book. Those articles are available online and are recommended reading as a supplement to this text (see the References section).[18] Robinson produced this book with only chapter numbers; I have added chapter titles to provide a sense of the flow of thought, and I have included in my titles a statement of Robinson's from within each chapter. I have also added subheads within the chapters; this and the afterword were at the suggestions of colleagues who read and contributed to this text. Robinson wrote without footnotes, so all notes to the text are written by me in an effort to clarify and document many of Robinson's statements.[19]

Robinson does not date his reflections, but by comparing his text with archival records it is possible to outline a rough chronology. His first chapter gives no location information, but roughly deals with his first two years in India, 1882–84.[20] Chapter 2 is about his time in Gubbi, which was in 1885; the focus is on the summer (April–May) outreach.[21] Chapter 3 is mainly reflections on the events of chapter 2, and ends with the completion of language exams, so is roughly the second half of 1885.[22] Chapter 4 tells stories from 1886, when

---

18. Earlier, in 1885, Robinson had also written about his itineration among villagers. That paper, under the pseudonym A. Vidyarthi, is also highly recommended reading and is available online (see Robinson 1885e for details). Besides the papers listed for Robinson in the References Cited section, he wrote two articles for *The Harvest Field* that do not directly relate to this book: "Samuel Caleb: A Faithful Hindu Minister," *The Harvest Field*, second series, vol. 6 no. 11, May 1886, 321-27; and "Mysore District Meeting 1888," *The Harvest Field*, second series, vol. 8 no. 8, Feb. 1888, 253-62. Posthumously, a copy of his collection of Sanskrit proverbs (in English, with no reference to the original sources) was also published: *Lotus Bloom from a Sanskrit Lake*, London: Charles H. Kelley, 1913.
19. I had originally decided to present these as endnotes so Robinson's text would remain more distinct, but in light of my numerous editorial changes to his text and in deference to the opinions of those who read the text for me, I finally opted for footnotes.
20. Robinson seems to have started in Mysore City, but was assigned to Chikmagalur in 1883. "We have therefore appointed Mr. Robinson to Chikmagalur—a station in which without distraction he may devote himself to the study of the language & the people & thus prepare himself for fruitful activity hereafter in any position that may be assigned to him" (UTC, "Minutes of the Mysore District Meeting Begun in Bangalore Dec. 29th 1882," in Synod Minutes 1877-1897, C37/B, MMS 21, 248). However, the Synod Minutes for Jan. 2, 1884, indicate that Robinson was still in Mysore City (UTC, "Minutes of the Mysore District Meeting Begun in Bangalore January 2, 1884," in Synod Minutes 1877-1897, C37/B, MMS 21, 259).
21. The 1885 synod minutes again suggest that Robinson is in Chikmagalur, yet they also put him in Gubbi along with John Mark; and as this is the only reference to Gubbi, it is certain that 1885 was his time there (UTC, "Minutes of the Mysore District Meeting Begun in Bangalore January 7th 1885," in Synod Minutes 1877-1897, C37/B, MMS 21, 294-95).
22. The three language exams were held on January 2, 1884, January 7, 1885, and January 4, 1886. See also note 88 on pg. 31.

Robinson was in Chikmagalur.²³ Chapter 5 consists of stories from 1887 to July of 1889 when Robinson was in Shimoga.²⁴ The events of chapter 6 take place in July 1889 and after.

In closing this introduction to a unique book, I feel a need to apologize to Benjamin Robinson. I willingly sit at his feet, and lean forward to touch his feet in deep subservience to his vision as outlined in this book. In my understanding, Robinson has intentionally presented a conundrum, with an approach that defies simple rational analysis. His book failed; it was rarely read, wrongly interpreted in light of a controversy about missionary lifestyles, and soon forgotten. I have reworked his message and provide commentary focused on rational analysis, seeking to explain what he (it seems to me) preferred to leave for intuitive assimilation. I am not sanguine about my method succeeding where his failed, but with deep humility toward one whom I would gladly own as a guru, I had to make the attempt.

—H. L. Richard
August 2019

---

23. The 1886 Synod Minutes once again indicate Robinson was at Chikmagalur (UTC, "Minutes of the Mysore District Meeting held in Bangalore Jan 4th 1886," in Synod Minutes 1877-1897, C37/B, MMS 21, 325); and his text (see pg. 34) seems to suggest he only started in Chikmagalur in 1886 after completing his language exams.
24. From 1887, Robinson was at Shimoga (UTC, "Minutes of the Mysore District Meeting held in Bangalore Jan 3rd 1887," in Synod Minutes 1877-1897, C37/B, MMS 21, 353).

Foreword to the 1st Edition by Henry Haigh

I responded very willingly to the author's request that I should write a brief introduction to his book. It was my privilege to know Mr. Robinson during the whole of his time in India. No man ever flung himself with greater zest and determination into the life, language, and thought of the people among whom he was appointed to labor. From the first India cast its spell over him in an extraordinary degree. Its languages were a challenge in which he delighted. He spared no labor, he shirked no difficulty. Root, stem, idiom—they were there to be mastered, and it was with him a point of honor, as well as a matter of desire, to master them. The philosophies of India received from him minute attention; critical always, but always reverent and sympathetic. Especially did the brooding mysticism of the East make congenial appeal to him.[25] He gave it free but discriminating access to his deepest nature, until he became saturated with it. Recognizing deep differences between himself and the people of his adoption and his love, he nevertheless discovered real and fundamental kinship. Thus it was easy for him to move about among them in kindly, sympathetic fashion. He put on no airs, he claimed no privilege as one of the conquering race. Everywhere he was the brother of the people, the friend who counts it his first privilege to help, the patient, modest teacher whose method it was to suggest and educe rather than dogmatically to affirm. So it became a passion with him to break down barriers, to reconcile differences, and to embody in his life the spirit of a true fraternity.

It was in this way that the author came to make the experiment of which, in part, this book is the story. The idea was not new. Other men, one here and another there, had in their degree made the attempt. But the general missionary judgement and practice in India were, and are, otherwise. Not with a desire to discount that judgement, and still less with a desire to be singular,

---

25. "The brooding mysticism of the East" is an Orientalist trope that has been exposed as simplistic and misguided by careful analysis; see especially Richard King's landmark study of *Orientalism and Religion: Postcolonial Theory, India and "The Mystic East"* (New Delhi: Oxford University Press, 1991).

did Mr. Robinson enter upon his path. But he was willing to do anything possible that might truly bridge the distance between himself and his people; and he thought he was in a singularly favorable position for making this particular attempt. No man ever adventured himself on an enterprise moved by more self-forgetting chivalry or truer Christian compassion. How it began, how proceeded, and how ended—it is all written in this book. Suffice for me to say that it proved a costly experiment. It not only compelled his return to England utterly broken in health, but its results have pursued him all through his ministry. They still abide, and it was during a recent period of enforced absence from regular ministerial work that this book was written.

For many years there was a hope that Mr. Robinson would give to the public the benefit of his experiences and reflections. I have myself repeatedly urged upon him the desirability of doing this. He shrank greatly from it; and when one reads the intimate narrative now at last made public, the shrinking is easily intelligible. The story seems to lay bare the deep inner workings of a consecrated soul, and it will be read, I am sure, with reverence, as well as with interest and profit.

But the "experiment" is only a part of the book, which throws many an instructive sidelight on Indian life and literature, as also on missionary problems and methods. I hope the book will be widely read. It ought to kindle the imagination and stir the heart of the church, and make the great mission question at once more real and more urgent to all who call Christ Lord. The atmosphere of the book is as truly Indian as it is Christian. Its story was begotten in love, and continued in suffering. This author, at any rate, has not "loved" his life, but for Christ's sake and the gospel's has "lost" it. But he has "kept" it, too, in the hearts and lives of many in India with whom he came into such close and loving touch. I trust that now, through this volume, the perfume of this broken box of ointment may spread to many other lives.

Chapter 1

The Beginning of Understanding and Conviction

How far does my life defile Christ's message?

–Benjamin Robinson

> Awe striking terror, vortex vast,
> Life's whirl must predetermine Caste,
> From highest God to lowest germs,
> The God have worship, writhe the worm.[26]

THE HAWK AND THE DOVE

The goodness of King Shibi breathed fragrance through the three worlds. The gods Indra and Agni resolved to test his devotion. Indra became a hawk, Agni a dove. Pursued by the hawk, the dove fled to the king, sheltered behind him, and craved his protection. He promised that he would give his own life rather than give it up to death. As he was speaking, the hawk claimed that the dove was created on purpose for his food, and belonged to him of divine right. The king said, "It is your bounden duty, your lawful right, and virtue to slay and eat, but I have given my word to this dove; cannot you seek some other and be happy?"

"No," said the hawk, "none is so sweet as that, and unless you give me an equal weight from your own royal person, I will not forgo my right."

"Very good," said Shibi. Scales were ordered, the dove put into one, flesh cut from the king's own body in the other, but they could not outweigh the dove.

---

26. This little rhyme cannot be traced on the Internet. It is presumably from the language-learning manual that Robinson used in his early years in India, so perhaps it is a translation of a Kannada saying or a local production in English. There are resonances with the great vision of chapter 11 of the Bhagavad Gita, but no particular verse suggests what is stated here.

Shibi placed his head to the sword. Then Indra and Agni flamed forth in their divine splendor, and set the seal of their blessing on his true devotion.[27]

So I read in early Kannada studies,[28] and pondered. Is the dove created on purpose to be food for the hawk? Is it the hawk's bounden duty, its lawful right, and its virtue to slay to eat? Does the birth-condition determine the life-function? Is the being of gods and kings so determined? Does caste mean birth-condition, which determines the custom, and right, of men inevitably? Is caste as divinely ordained as the right of the hawk to slay and eat?

The divine law[29] teaches that the vast vortex of created life, which is terrible beyond words, and ever passes through becoming, growth, and death, includes all—from Brahma, the highest divinity, down to the lowest plant-germs. The Most Glorious, who is above speech and thought, for the sake of preserving all this creation ordained distinctive duties for those who sprang from His mouth, arm, thigh, and foot.[30] The deeds of men that spring from mind, or voice, or body bear fruit of bliss or woe. Through faulty deeds of the body, man reaches plants; through those of the voice, birds or wild animals; through those of the mind, low birth-condition. If goodness constitutes the chief element of being, divinity is reached; if passion, manhood; if darkness, animal forms.[31]

Caste

I read such words. Something of their meaning dawned upon me. I had thought of universal right binding upon all men. Eternal and unchangeable in principle. Pure, sober, kindly, godly lives would surely witness that to every Kannadiga man. A friend, an assistant commissioner in Mysore, told me that one night when camped out, as he sat in his tent he heard the Kannadiga

---

27. This is a common folktale that appears in the Mahābhārata epic a few times; see 3.131, van Buitenen 1975, 470f. Robinson's conclusion praising King Shibi's "devotion" (*bhakti*) is intriguing, as the story rather highlights his commitment to truth or to dharma. See my introductory comments on Robinson's failure to recognize the centrality of *bhakti* to living Hindu traditions (pg. xxvii–xxviii).
28. Robinson used here and in many other places the antiquated term *Kanarese*, which I have replaced throughout with the now-standard *Kannada* (referring to the dominant language spoken in the state of Karnataka) or *Kannadiga* (the people who speak the Kannada language).
29. This presumably refers to dharma.
30. This is clearly a reference to the Puruṣasūkta, Rig Veda 10:90, particularly verse 12 on the creation of the four *varnas* from mouth, arm, thigh, and foot of the Cosmic Man. Note that the Rig Veda makes no association of different occupations related to these four social groups, about which the author of the hymn assumes basic knowledge. (See also note 38 in this chapter.)
31. This is a reasonable summary of some Upanishadic teaching, like Bṛhadāraṇyaka U. 4.4 or Chāndogya U. 5.10.7, or the Bhagavad Gita 14.5–20, etc.

men outside say, "This *sahib*[32] doesn't say ____, doesn't drink brandy. What can he be?"

One deep-thoughted man solved it by saying, "Why this *sahib* must belong to the missionary caste."

The Lingāyats are bearers of the Linga, the god Siva's most sacred symbol, on their breasts. Brāhmans count them as heretics.[33] Once their faith was the state religion of Mysore.[34] Talking with one of their spiritual directors (gurus) in the courts of a temple, I asked him where, if I wished to become his disciple, he could teach me, and on what conditions I could be received into their community. He said, "If you complied with our conditions, received our teaching, and after probation were approved, we could receive you into our religion (our system of religious thought), but into our caste—never; that is impossible."[35]

As he used the word *jāti*—which we render caste, the constitution with which and the condition into which one is born—he spoke with reverent awe and a depth of meaning I could not then fathom. The meaning and mystery of caste began to unfold.

---

32. *Sahib* is an Urdu term (from Persian) meaning lord or master, commonly used by Indians toward all Europeans during the colonial era.
33. The concept of "heresy" in Hindu traditions hardly exists in the Christian sense of a teaching that violates orthodox standards. There is no single Hindu orthodoxy; there is a rubric where distinctions are made between *āstika* and *nāstika*, often defined as "believing" and "unbelieving," usually with the added note that it is believing or not believing the Vedas that is the distinguishing issue. The Lingāyats rejected the Vedas, probably the reason why Robinson's Brāhman friends referred to them as heretics. (See also note 35 of this chapter.)
34. The *Imperial Gazetteer of India* states this, particularly dating the supremacy of Lingāyatism in Mysore from 1350 to 1610 (Cotton et al, 1908, 202).
35. Robinson is touching on the complex relationship between caste and *sampradāya* (sect, tradition, theology), and is assuming too much of an assimilation between the two. The Lingāyats are a multi-caste confessional movement that was originally an anti-caste movement; today they often function like a caste but maintain aspects of a *sampradāya* (community based on a traditional teaching). See Schouten 1995 on the Lingāyats, and see A. M. Shah's seminal paper on the neglect of "sects" (*sampradāyas*) in the study and understanding of Hindu traditions (Shah 2006). The greatest change in this area in recent decades is the shift to conversions to Hinduism, a trend begun by the Hare Krishna movement which gradually has been assimilated by more mainstream Hindu traditions (Julia Roberts being a recent Hollywood convert to Hinduism). The caste status of such people is one of many complexities related to outsiders converting to Hinduism. (See Venkatesan Vembu's satirical piece about Julia Roberts' caste at http://www.dnaindia.com/analysis/column-dear-julia-roberts-1423112.)

Three Types of Brāhmans

Often Brāhmans are grouped together as one caste. In Karnataka there are three great series of castes among them. The Smārtas, followers of the sacred *smriti*, the traditional interpretation of scripture, worship Siva. In religious thought they are *advaitins* (i.e., non-dualists), holding that the only real substance is one, alone; all that appears is in truth only seeming. They bear three white ashen marks drawn horizontally through a round spot on the forehead, across each breast, and three times on each arm. The Mādhavas, who are followers of Madhvāchārya, taught exactly the opposite. They are *dvaitas*, or dualists, and maintain the eternal difference of finite selves from Vishnu, the great Supreme. They bear a vertical black mark drawn through a black, round spot above the nose, and the seal of Vishnu on forehead, breast, and arms. The Srivaishnavas bear the trident in the middle of the forehead—the center line red and the two outer ones white. They worship Vishnu, and in religious thought they are modified non-dualists, holding that the distinction of creator and created must subsist eternally, excepting that finite selves may gain closest unity with the divine.

The facial expression and bearing of each of these three castes is as different from each other as their caste marks and religious systems of thought.[36] A Smārta friend once said to me that the Mādhavas worshipped Hanuman,[37] the monkey-god, until they became monkey-headed; that they insisted on duality until it developed self-assertion to excess, while his own non-dual system led to a truer sense of proportion as to the relative value of the individual ego. My teacher was a Srivaishnava, who bore the honorific title *Ayyangāra*. I had a friend who was called a Srivaishnava, wore the same caste marks, and bore the priestly title *Acharya*. In the course of our study the differences of caste among Brāhmans was suggested. I said, "Is not _____ *Acharya* one of your own caste?"

"Certainly not," he said. "For the sake of influence and position we should pay deference to him, but really we could not own him as of our caste."

---

36. Certainly there were differences among these Brāhman groups in theological system and in "caste marks" (an antiquated term referring to forehead markings, which often included even those that have nothing to do with caste, like the simple *bindi* (dot) that is worn as makeup by most modern Indian women). But that one could tell what type of Brāhman a person was by their "facial expression and bearing" seems hyperbolic (at best). Robinson's descriptions of the teachings of these groups is valid, but the issue raised in the previous note comes into play; Srivaiṣṇavism is not a Brāhman group but a sampradāya with distinctive beliefs and practices which are maintained by many non-Brāhmans as well as Brāhmans. Mādhva Brāhman theology is rightly defined, but among Mādhva Brāhmans today there are many who care little for philosophy/theology, but merely maintain a caste identity.
37. Robinson's original text reads "Hanumanta," also in a later reference.

So one began to learn that each of the three great castes of Brāhmans was divided into many castes which could not become one.[38]

The Brāhman's birth is the everlasting[39] essential form of dharma—duty, right, virtue.[40] He is born for the sake of dharma, and exists for the divine scripture. His heart is the home of prayer. He is guardian of the scripture, and of its sacred powers; he alone can lead to the highest. That ideal has been written into the very life-texture of the worthy Brāhman. Wide and deep as are the differences among themselves, the difference between them and all other castes is far wider and deeper. I have seen a Brāhman woman, scowling, hiss a lad of another caste away from her, so that he should not come within the proscribed distance, and his presence defile. A dalit[41] coming along a public bridge saw a Brāhman coming from the other end of the bridge; he turned back, and went off the road, lest in crossing the bridge he should come within defiling distance.[42]

The Complexity of Caste

The other castes, heretics, and dalits baffled and bewildered me by their number and deep differences. Each is a complex series of castes which cannot become one. Each insists upon its own caste rights as divine and unalterable for all within its circle. The unclean dalits—who must live apart, outside town or village—would no more tolerate the presence of a Brāhman in their parts than a Brāhman would tolerate them in a Brāhman street.

But the differences between the castes themselves seemed to me then little compared with the gulf between them all and myself. With all my heart I wished to be helpful to everyone, and, if it might be, lead them to the truest manhood and to God. Every day one saw the gulf deepen, broaden.

---

38. There is potential confusion here related to the fact that "caste" is used to translate two different Sanskrit terms. *Varna* is the simpler term, as there are only four *varnas* and all Brāhmans by definition share the Brāhman *varna*. But Robinson is mostly referring to *jāti*, which is a more dynamic term, as there is no set number of *jātis* and there are many Brāhman *jātis*.
39. Robinson used the antiquated term "ever-during."
40. What exactly Robinson means by saying that the Brāhman's "birth" is the "essential form of dharma" is not clear to me or to those I have consulted about this matter. The status and enjoined behavior of the Brāhman points to the ideals of Hindu life or dharma; this seems to be the point.
41. Robinson used the dated term "outcaste." Here and throughout his text I substitute the modern term "dalit," which means the broken or oppressed.
42. Urbanization in India has brought drastic change in this area. Note that much had already changed by Robinson's time, as the earlier practice of "unseeability" had ceased (see Hutton 1961, 81).

Once, before daybreak, I lay down on a flat rock overlooking Gersoppa Falls. Spray and mist arose from the depths, I could not see the bottom, and shuddering terror seized me. As day dawned, I saw into the depths, and the awful rocks of the vast chasm grew clear. Then I toiled down the steep cliffs nearly to the lower water-bed. As I looked upward and around, the whole scene, so far above words, seemed to possess me.

"The Question of My Life"

So, and yet much more, seemed the vasty deep between the castes and myself. In the beginning of my second year I spent two days at the Lingāyat temple festival at Yediyuru [Yedeyur]. Ten thousand worshippers came together. Men lying on beds of sharp thorns; men with their heads buried in the ground; Vaishnava priests with gong and shell of maddening din; shepherd priests with bearskin garb; men and women prostrating themselves in the dust for a full half-mile to the river, bathing, then returning to the temple, every step a prostration, to present their hair as an offering to their god—these and many other weird sights live in my memory still.

We kept on teaching and talking as we could in the ceaseless noise of the crowd until late at night. The moonlight was like milk poured on the ground. I left the crowd, and went to the travelers' rest-house nearby for the night. But not to sleep. The sounds of the festival kept alive in me all the scenes of the day. From the shouts of ten thousand throats when the ponderous sacred cart began to creak and sway and move,[43] to the talk of the man who asked me if I could defy gravitation by my spirit-force—it was all there.

How far away the people in spirit! It was as if every conversation only made one feel the depths between us more and more. The next night I rode home alone. Between snatches of sleep the whole scene was still with me, seemingly more vivid than in the daylight. Could I by any wise means get near to the heart of my brothers, so that one's life might help them to feel the meaning of a common Father's love? That became thenceforward the question of my life.

Imperialism and a Gospel of Service

That leads to another question. Are the manners and bearing of a ruling race, the power to command, with all the deep and subtle influence which that exerts upon personality, helpful to one who wishes to lead men, so different

---

43. The "carts" or "chariots" (*rath*) of gods of major temples are pulled through their towns in annual festivals. The most famous of these is in Puri, Odisha (see http://rathjatra.nic.in/), where the pulling of the massive chariot of Jagannatha led to the English term "juggernaut."

from himself, into the fellowship of the meek and lowly One? I remembered what He said of the rulers who lord it over their subjects. "Ye shall not be so"; "I came not to receive, but to render service"; "Learn of Me, for I am meek and lowly in heart."

Such words grew in power within me till I could only wrestle in prayer for grace to obey. The John Bull[44] within me urged, "Have not you the same right to your birth-constitution and condition as they to theirs?" But there was ever present within me One Presence. I could see no form, but I felt somehow wound into me the life-and-death meaning of His meekness, His cross.[45]

Challenging Encounters

A Lingāyat priest came to my study. We had a long talk on religion. Then he said, "Would you please let me see your sacred book?"

I handed a Bible to him. He shrank back in horror such as I never knew before, and gasping, said, "*charma* (leather)!"

All unwittingly, I had offered him a leather-bound Bible. To him to touch leather was the most unthinkable and defiling abomination. I could have sunk into the earth for shame, and earnestly besought him to pardon me, and believe that I did it in ignorance, not with intent to defile.

But the question then came thus—What if I myself and my mode of life be as abominable to those whom I wish to teach and help as the leather to the Lingāyat? I wished to hand him the Word of God, and it was bound in an abomination that he could not come near. The choking answer came—eating flesh, especially beef, is more abominable still.

At another festival we were waiting aside until the excitement of the crowd at the presence of the god in his palanquin had ceased.[46] A man sitting near us,

---

44. Ben Johnson, in an article on John Bull on a British history website, states that "John Bull is an imaginary figure who is a personification of England, similar to the American 'Uncle Sam'" (http://www.historic-uk.com/CultureUK/John-Bull/).
45. The inherent contradictions of "colonial Christianity" are insightfully pointed out here. Robinson had no possibility of transcending this historical embarrassment; to this day church and mission thought and practice have not yet come close to adequate repudiation of colonialism and its heritage. For a powerful presentation of this problem, focused on Punjab in north India, see Jeffrey Cox's *Imperial Fault Lines: Christianity and Colonial Power in India, 1838-1940*.
46. The online Oxford dictionary entry for *palanquin* says, "(In India and the East) a covered litter for one passenger, consisting of a large box carried on two horizontal poles by four or six bearers" (https://www.lexico.com/en/definition/palanquin). Here it is a god (*murti*, image) being carried around, a scaled-down version of what is described in note 43 on the previous page.

who had listened to our preaching, said to me, "How can you expect your teaching to have any effect when you yourself disobey your own scripture?"

"How so?" I said.

"Your scripture says, 'Take off thy shoes from off thy feet, for the place whereon thou standest is holy ground,' and you enter your temple with boots on."

I was startled again. Such direct criticism was sharp, if healing, and I was compelled to question deeper still—How far does my life defile Christ's message?

Life Is Sacred

Whatever differences may exist between Brāhmans and all who acknowledge their sacred position, or between them and Lingāyats and Jains, all are agreed that to take life for food is the greatest sin of all sins, and that to slay the bullock for food is the most grievous of all deadly sins. The unbeginning past of life determines the present sheath of life, but all life is essentially the same. Trees and plants are conscious life. A man will not cut down a tree without worship, sometimes will defer cutting for months lest if cut down untimely, the life hurt there should bring harm to his own home.

But the reverence for the bull and the cow cannot be expressed. Slaughter of cows is worse even than slaughter of Brāhmans, divine as they are. The bull is sacred to Siva, and even among the worshippers of Vishnu there is the same deep reverence for the cow. Thus it is that the deepest and most sacred religious feeling of all those castes is outraged by eating beef. The Jain will not eat food by oil light, lest insects or flies should burn in its flame. To tread upon ant or creeping thing is a serious sin.

Embracing Local Ways in Dress and Diet

It was clear to me, then, that one could not adopt the custom or dress of every caste; they were too many, various, and contradictory.[47] It seemed doubtful if any custom or any dress could be adopted in its entirety. But as I learned and felt how abominable leather was, and how sacrilegious flesh-eating was, the question was narrowed to—Is it my duty to give up eating flesh-meat

---

47. Note that many lower castes have always eaten meat, and today only a minority of Hindus are pure vegetarians; this is part of the various and contradictory customs Robinson refers to. The Anthropological Survey of India data from the 1980s demonstrated this point: "The data generated by the People of India [research] suggests that contrary to the general impression and in spite of the higher value attached to vegetarianism, only about 20 percent of Indian communities are vegetarian" (Singh 1992, 64).

entirely, and to wear the cotton waist-cloth and sandals? Will the avoiding of those things that plainly outrage sacred feelings help me better to commend my message as a minister of Christ?

I read the Abbé Dubois' account of his experiment in that direction. It was clear that, for whatever reason, he gained great influence; but after thirty years' service, he said he did not think it possible for a Hindu to become a true Christian![48] His example had been before our own missionaries in Karnataka for fifty years. Many of them must have thought through the same question, but not one of them, so far as I knew, had tried to live on the food of Kannadiga men, or wear any form of un-English dress.

The sincerity and devotion of many of these men claimed and received my reverence. Was it wise or respectful for me to do what such devoted men, after mature knowledge and thought, had quite deliberately declined to do? Was it not, rather, an impertinence to adopt a form of life which would single me out from a brotherhood of which I was, and wished to be, a loyal member? I knew that, for many, considerations of health made any such experiment undesirable, if not absolutely impossible.

---

48. The claim that the Abbé J. A. Dubois (1765-1848) gained great influence among Hindus is debatable, and Robinson's comment "for whatever reason" seems to suggest some doubts. The Abbé wrote that:

> I had no sooner arrived amongst the natives of India than I recognized the absolute necessity of gaining their confidence. Accordingly, I made it my constant rule to live as they did. I adopted their style of clothing, and I studied their customs and methods of life in order to be exactly like them.... By such circumstances I was able to ensure a free and hearty welcome from people of all castes and conditions ... (Dubois and Beauchamp 1906, 8)

But recent scholarship has concluded that Dubois' work was mainly plagiarized from Father Gaston Laurent Coeurdoux (App 2010, 397, referencing Murr 1987), raising more than a few doubts about this testimony of his wide acceptance among Hindus. Regarding the impossibility of winning Hindus to Christ, Dubois' words are clear:

> In fact, the conversion of the Hindoos, under existing circumstances, is so hopeless a thing, and their prejudices against it are so deeply rooted, and so decidedly declared, that I am firmly persuaded, that if (what has never been the case) the Hindoo Brahmins were animated by a spirit of proselytism, and sent to Europe missionaries of their own faith, to propagate their monstrous religion, and make converts to the worship of Seeva and Vishnoo, they would have much more chance of success, among certain classes of society, than we have to make among them true converts to the faith in Christ. (Dubois 1995[1823], 135-36; spelling as in the original)

I consulted my chairman, whose memory I revere.[49] He would not forbid it, as I felt so strongly; but he could not advise it, alike on account of the risk to health, and because he was doubtful if it would be of such service as I thought. I fully appreciated the risk to health, and I shrank from singularity in dress, and from all that it involved. I had no wish to be rash, or to earn any sort of notoriety, and I weighed carefully everything that was said to me. But in the end I could not either stifle or banish the conviction that I ought to change my dress and to live without flesh food.

During the remainder of that year I gradually lessened the amount of flesh food, so as to avoid any risk from sudden change. The next year I was appointed to Gubbi, where Thomas Hodson began our mission to the Kannadiga people and where William Arthur lived.[50] To me it was sacred ground. I was there alone, with a Kannadiga evangelist. Our first Kannada mission station was then, and until recently, a serious problem. The apparent results of so much devoted toil were meager and unsatisfactory. I could not expect that where so much earnest labor had produced no higher spiritual results, anything I could do would be of more effect. Yet I longed intensely to reach and win the hearts of men for Christ.

By day or night that desire never ceased its persistent pressure. Those lonely nights banished sleep. Sometimes the sainted dead, the men who began there without a hymn, without a convert for years, seemed to make their presence felt. Then the tens of thousands around, whose need was so deep and sore, crowded upon my thought. Could I cross the gulf, down its rugged steep, through its rocky torrent, and up the other side? I thought all through as sanely as I could, and felt I must try; I could not help it, I could do no other. So far as I know, I thought and acted sincerely, and with true-hearted devotion, wishing only to be the servant of the meek and lowly Lord in the service of men. In that spirit, I vowed, "I will."[51]

---

49. This was Josiah Hudson (1840-96), some of whose opinions about Robinson are given in appendix 2 related to Robinson's marriage.
50. The stories of Hodson's pioneering leadership (he started the WMMS work in Karnataka and served in India for forty-four years) and Arthur's brief sojourn in Gubbi (cut short by health issues; he was a secretary of the WMMS from 1851-68) are told in Findlay and Holdsworth 1924, 203-12. Robinson was in Gubbi in 1885 (see note 22 of the Introduction).
51. The incidents and struggles briefly outlined here were presented with a bit more detail in an article Robinson anonymously wrote for *The Harvest Field* in 1889 (Robinson 1889a). The only difference in perspective between the earlier article and this later book chapter is that some very strong language against practices in the Hindu festivals in the article is softened in this later account. The article is available online (see the References Cited section for details) and is highly recommended reading for further glimpses into the life and thought of Benjamin Robinson.

Chapter 2

Experiences in Contextual Evangelism[52]

It seemed at the end as if one were only beginning to see a little of the depth and width of the gulf.

—Benjamin Robinson

Give self to learn thought-baffling thought,
Search all Caste's subtle source has wrought.[53]

ITINERANT EVANGELISM

I had as colleague at Gubbi a trusted Kannadiga evangelist, John Mark.[54]

---

52. "Contextual" in this sense came into missionary use only in the early 1970s; its use here is an intentional reminder that these chapter titles were not Robinson's (as noted on pg. xxx of the Introduction), but were added to assist the understanding of twenty-first century readers.
53. See note 26 on page 1.
54. This was in 1885 (see note 22 of the Introduction). John Mark appears in the archival record a number of times. He began work with the WMMS in 1873, and his work alongside Robinson in Gubbi is noted (UTC, "Minutes of the Mysore District Meeting Begun in Bangalore January 7th 1885," in Synod Minutes 1877-1897, C37/B, MMS 21, 295-96). His testimony is recorded related to his examination for ordination ("examination of candidates for the native ministry"):

> John Mark says: I was born a heathen and baptized without any special desire on my part in 1862. In 1869 while still a boy, Mr. Dalzell sent me to the Tumkur Boarding School. I stayed here for two years & during that time was carefully instructed in Divine truth by Mr. John Stephenson. One Sunday when he preached on repentance I trembled & left the place much distressed. I continued in this state of mind 8 days and then found peace by believing in Jesus. Soon after I began to speak of the love of Jesus to my friends & others & felt something that told me that I ought to give myself to the work of preaching. (UTC, "Minutes of the Mysore District Meeting Begun in Bangalore January 7th 1885," in Synod Minutes 1877-1897, C37/B, MMS 21, 420).

Ordination was denied at that time, probably due to a weak sermon that was also part of the examination process. However, in 1889 John Mark was unanimously recommended for ordination (UTC, "Journal of Meetings for Mysore District," in Journal 1879-1923 Minutes, C38/B, MMS 27, 1889, 163).

I told him my purpose. He demurred. "No one else had tried to do this. If my health failed, might not the synod blame him?" In such ways he set all the reasons he could against my proposal, with an earnestness I could not then understand. I told him I had thought it all through. When at last he reluctantly assented, I asked him to buy me several loincloths,[55] such as are ordinarily worn, and a pair of sandals; to engage a bullock cart from one of our young Christian farmers, and an orphan boy to go with him to cook for him such food—excepting only flesh—as he would eat himself, and which I would share. We then arranged a tour of about six weeks, through villages away from the main roads, where missionary or evangelist seldom went.

We had with us a small tent, a few books, and as few other things as could be. No chair or table, no crockery or cutlery, just a bell-metal vessel or two for use at meals. I hoped it would be possible after inuring myself in this way to the simplest life, thereafter to visit villages to teach and help without carrying any luggage whatever. Ordinarily we pitched our tent only on a Saturday, so as to have quiet and retirement for worship and prayers. On other nights we usually slept on the ground.

We arose before daybreak, and arranged where the cart should go, so that we might join it at noon. Then we set forth, calling at all the villages we came to, teaching and talking as we found opportunity. Having reached our cart, we dined under such shade as could be found, studied till about three o'clock, dispatched the cart to the next place, and visited more villages. After reaching our appointed rendezvous, we had the evening meal, and then flung ourselves on the ground, in the hope that, as the Kannadigas say, sleep would come to us.

The sun soon blistered, skinned, and then tanned my exposed limbs. First attempts at walking barefoot were very painful, especially on broken quartz; but I persevered until I was able to walk fourteen miles before breakfast without hurt.[56] I fear I shrank from the curious, challenging gaze of the people, and from their comments—loud and sometimes rude—about an English missionary walking thus.

---

55. This is not a happy term for what Robinson elsewhere calls the *panche* (1889a, 365), another term for *dhoti* (see https://www.utsavpedia.com/attires/panche-the-essence-of-karnataka/, for a description and pictures), which is certainly not a loincloth, but there is not an adequate English descriptor.
56. Literally barefoot seems extreme and unnecessary, but is affirmed on page 21. See appendix 3 for contemporary debates about missionary lifestyles, including going barefoot.

I practiced eating with my fingers until I could do it dexterously, shooting the rice into the mouth without missing a grain. It was harder to learn to drink respectably—that is, to convey the water to one's mouth in a steady stream without letting the vessel touch one's lips. How constantly and humiliatingly it *would* gurgle back through my nostrils! I never saw bread or tea, or any form of English food, during these weeks. At first rice or ragi (millet) and vegetable curry did not seem unpalatable as prepared in the Kannadiga way; but after a while visions of bread and butter kept returning to tantalize me.[57]

After about a month, when the sun burned fiercer every day and the baked ground relentlessly flung back its waxing heat every night,[58] I was tempted sorely to question if it were worthwhile, and if it could be endured. I had feared lest the constant exposure to the glare would hurt my eyes. Happily, they grew accustomed to the blazing light and heat. The internal organs did not grow accustomed to the food. Once we had had a long forenoon walk, and taught in several villages. There were but few trees near our resting place, and they cast but poor shade. I sat under one of them, tired and worn. As I thought of the food that was coming, everything within me revolted against it, and there came such a sense of nausea as I hope never to know again. A dry crust would have been bread from heaven to me then. How to conceal what I felt, and make pretense to eat, I did not know. At first it seemed as if I could not face the walk and work we had planned for the evening. Will conquered feeling, however, and I ate—how I know not, but I hope without sign to my companion of the awful revolt within. At three o'clock we started for our six-mile walk and teaching. Many times I had to fight against such inward revolt, but it never really became a hurtless task.

Food and Caste

Several times during our journey people offered us food. I had thought and hoped perchance they might allow us to eat in their homes, but that was never suggested. Once a clean outer room was offered us, in which to eat the food given to us, but it was never even supposed they or we could think of anything

---

57. This comment reveals how rarely missionaries at the time ate a local diet. How ironic that Indian food is now popular across the world! Clearly Robinson was eating the rough food of the poor, and hindsight is clear that he should have eaten a higher standard of Indian diet.
58. This suggests that Robinson's experiment was carried out during the summer, again a strange decision that helps account for his breakdown. This impression is confirmed in Robinson's 1889 article which states that "it was the hot weather" when this trip was undertaken (1889a, 365). This would have been April-May of 1885 (see the first line of the following chapter which indicates this was a seven week trip; the last sentence of the first paragraph of this chapter says "about six weeks").

other than eating apart and out of sight. Once a cool place near a stream was pointed out to us as a convenient place to eat some plantains given to us.

I learned during those weeks, as I could not have learned otherwise, the sacredness of food to the Brāhman and others. A meal is a sacrifice in the most sacred sense. Food must only be eaten when ceremonially purified, with the whole self concentrated in the Divine. Food itself must ever be worshipped. The sight of my eyes falling upon a Brāhman's food would defile it. A grain of rice touching the lips and falling back would defile the rest.

I saw a Brāhman purified for the noon meal. We talked about the scripture for some time, but at such a distance that he should not be defiled. Once a Brāhman was speaking to me about the necessity of a good understanding between Briton and Brāhman. I said I wished it were possible that we could have social intercourse at table. His emphatic, "That could never be—impossible!" taught me that even the thought of such intercourse created horror.[59] This truth I gained: that food is a family sacrifice, to which birth alone gives right of place, and that however I dressed, or whatever I ate, I could not in this life gain that birthright.

Attitudes in the Villages

A little of the meaning of the life of Kannadiga villages entered into me deeply then. The condition of the children appeared to me pitiable—irresponsible in their seemingly almost wild freedom, yet bound by caste without hope of freedom from that. In many villages there was a most urgent appeal for a school. They had no money, but would give grain to the teachers. How often I was grieved by refusing, because we had no money for more schools!

An absolute sense of unalterable destiny rules their thought. To every appeal to arouse themselves toward a better manhood, there was one answer: "Such life is for you, but it is written on our foreheads that we much scratch the ground and live on such grain as we can grow."[60] Sometimes I used to

---

59. Food and eating continue to carry vastly more "theological" significance among Hindus than among Christians, but the extremes described by Robinson have changed as globalization necessitates a degree of intercourse that makes old taboos impossible to maintain. Noted twenty-first century Hindu scholar Arvind Sharma, in a discussion of this topic, sides with Benjamin Robinson that inter-dining with and between castes and communities would be a great step forward for Indian society. Sharma closes his discussion by asking the question, "Could it be that the way of establishing both intracommunal and intercommunal harmony in India may be as simple as that—let all dine together?" (2017, 320).
60. That one's fate is written on their forehead continues to be referenced in India, yet the notion is without basis in Hindu scripture. See Eliza Kent (2009) for an analysis that subverts the traditional fatalistic understanding.

think they were simply trying to evade the appeal out of lazy acquiescence in their condition, and because they did not wish to be troubled to make any upward effort. I think now it was rather the sense of the binding duty of reverence for the ancestral customs into which they were born and of awe in the presence of divine destiny working through all the past in determining the present.[61]

Some of the marriage ceremonies which I saw, and where I received the betel[62] given to the guests on arriving, were deeply interesting; but when I asked the meaning of any part of the ceremony, "custom" was the reply. The ignorance of some of the Brāhmans amazed and pained me. One of them asked, "What can we do now that the Veda has come into your hands?" Then, in a kind of angered grief, he said to his son, "You must learn from this *sahib* now."[63]

Many asked questions about our religious teaching, which showed earnest thought and a wish to learn. Again and again we were asked why we had never brought such word before, and when we would come again. Sometimes we were treated rudely, sometimes shown, plainly but politely, that we were not wanted. Several times we were asked why we came there in such a way. Why didn't we keep the main road? Why didn't we have a chariot and servants? What was the real purpose of our visit? When we said that we came to teach the true way that leads from sin to the one true God, we were greeted with an incredulous shrug. "Oh, dear no; you must have some ulterior aim. Are you seeing where schools are needed, or what are you doing for the government?"

More than once it was said with a kind of churlish insinuation that we were defrauding them. "Other sahibs have come with horses and servants. Why do you come in this poverty-stricken way?" Through it all I was patiently and carefully studying the bearing of everything I saw and learned upon my main purpose and problem. The difficulty of the problem grew upon me daily.

---

61. Village life has changed! The "unchanging village" of the nineteenth-century imagination, very clearly seen in a statement in *The Harvest Field* in 1885, was always a myth: "By gazing on the India of to-day we can imagine perfectly the surroundings of the people who lived here three thousand years ago" (Sawday 1885, 324). See Inden 1990, 131-34, for this myth of the unchanging Indian village, and its refutation.
62. Betel (*pān* in north India) is a heart-shaped leaf which is folded with various ingredients inside, often including tobacco, and chewed. It is often given to an honored guest or to those who attend a special function.
63. On *sahib*, see note 32 on page 3. This story is also told in Robinson 1885e, 143.

A Temple Festival

We spent three days in the midst of the ten thousand people who came to the Yediyuru temple festival,[64] which I had seen from the outside a year before. Our tent was in the midst of the crowd. Audiences and questioners were never wanting, except when the great car of Siddhalingéshvare[65] was drawn at noon.

Once two elderly men spoke out of the ring around us, and said, "Why, sir, we repeat 'Our Father' every day."

I said, "Are you Christians, then?"

"Oh, no; we could not become Christians. We should be put out of caste, and that would be worse than death."

"When you say, 'Thy will be done, etc.'" I asked, "does it not mean that you should obey the Lord Jesus and follow Him fully?"

"Sir," they said, "we have given up worshipping material forms; we bend as we were taught in your school to our Father. Don't you think God must think us worthy of much reward because we do so much?"

One man wished to test my right to teach. "Can you introduce a clean cloth down your throat into your inside and draw it out again as clean as when it went in?"

When I said I had never made that experiment, he said, "Seems to me you're not much of a teacher. Ours are as pure as that, and can do wondrous things."

When the sun went down, we still kept on at our task. Then the people began to get their food, and we had ours. The clear moon shone upon everything so clearly that we could read without strain, and it gave to the whole scene a tender setting. There was weird yet attractive music near our tent, and I saw one of the most graceful, simple dances, where sticks were touched in the winding round to the time of the music.[66]

---

64. Most Hindu temples, even down to rather small shrines, have an annual festival. Related to important temples, these become significant regional festivals. For info on the Yediyuru Lingāyat Shiva temple, see http://www.karnataka.com/bangalore/kunigal-yediyuru-siddhalingeshwara-swamy-temple/.
65. See note 43 on page 6 on the temple carts. Siddhalingeshwara was a fifteenth-century Lingāyat saint who wrote numerous poems (*vachanas*) (Schouten 1995, 67f.).
66. "Weird" is not politically correct by modern standards, and it is odd that it is linked with "attractive." Robinson does not seem to have studied the music of Karnataka, and he would have benefitted by following out the implications of his suggestion that this music was attractive.

I was allowed to enter the temple court—barefoot, of course—and studied forms of worship there. I tried hard to see all I could, to learn all I could; but it seemed at the end as if one were only beginning to see a little of the depth and width of the gulf.

Challenges on the Road

Our cart had many a strain, and was turned over more than once. We had one road begun as a famine relief work, and left unfinished. It was worse than the country tracks worn by wheels and rain. There was much scrub-jungle, and several village names were preceded by "tiger." The whole scene suggested them. We had two most interested audiences in the morning. They were very shy of us at first. The women beat their mouths,[67] and hastened out of sight. One by one we drew the men near, and their intelligent concern about religion was most cheering.

In the afternoon we told the bullock boy to meet us at "Tiger Hill," some few miles along the road, and we went to two villages off the road. Intelligent questioning after our teaching detained us, so that twilight was gone as we left the last village. It was full moon. The country was lonely and noiseless, save for jackals. The silence was only broken by our voices. John Mark said, "What if a tiger comes, sir?"

I said, "We must pray to Daniel's God."

But as the distance grew, and we were tired, it was trying to both of us. After a long while we heard the welcome bark of a dog, and found our boys asleep outside the village. When they could be roused, they said they were tired, and had cooked no food, as the headman of the village gave food to all who asked. He ploughed twenty yoke of oxen, had fingers covered with gold, and always gave food. John Mark said, "Their rice is coarser than our ragi, and you could never bear their burning-hot curry."

I said I would try, and anyhow we must have that or fast at that hour. The food was given. They would not suffer us to draw water from the village well, lest our vessels should defile it, but were good enough to draw water for us in their own vessels and pour it into ours. They were Sudras, the fourth caste, whose only duty is service to the first three. When the food came, one was glad to test one's power. It was as if a mustard plaster had been applied all

---

67. Women "beating their mouths" is highly inauspicious, an action taken at the death of a child, the sudden loss of property, or other disastrous or forbidden acts.

down one's throat, and the whole inner organism smarted the next morning. We lay down to rest on the hillside near the village. I watched the eclipse of the moon, and listened to the wild music of the village, which they thought might help the moon out of the jaws of the monster Rahu.[68]

In the morning we went to call upon the headman, to thank him for his hospitality. We found him in the fields nearby. As we made salaams [greetings], he eyed us as if he would search us through. His manner was as obtrusively overbearing as his many gold rings. Before we could thank him, he scowlingly asked what we were doing there. I said we had come to thank him for his kindness of the night before.

Heedless of our thanks, he said, "But why do you go about the country like this?"

I replied that we wished to teach the true way of deliverance from sin. Then, in unconcealed anger, he exclaimed, "Sin! Do you mean to tell *me* of my sin? I feed twenty persons every night of my life. Is not that more than enough to balance my sin? What deliverance do I need? No, no; that is not all."

I studied the man and his thought as I said, "We have no other purpose than to lead men to the grace of God, our Father in Jesus Christ."

"Oh," cried he, "I thought perhaps you might have come to see what villages need schools. But why did you not come dressed like other sahibs?"

He then began insinuations of vile motives, and would not even receive my thanks.

At a Village School

Another day, at noon, we rested by a clear stream running between silvery sand banks, with a few shady trees, near a village where a number of Jains live. These are closely akin to Buddhists in thought and practice.

---

68. Anthony Stone defines Rahu and the corresponding Ketu:

> In present day astrology, Rahu and Ketu are the "nodes" of the moon's orbit, which are the two points in the sky where the moon's path crosses the path of the sun. Rahu is the "ascending node" where the moon moves to the north of the sun's path, and Ketu is the "descending node" where the moon moves to the south. (1981, 25)

> This lies behind the myth that Rahu is a monster who tries to "swallow the sun or moon at eclipses" (ibid., 27).

Buddhism was quenched in, or driven out of, its homeland by persecution.[69] The exact relation of the Jains to Gautama [Buddha] is unknown, but they survived in Karnataka, where they once had great influence. Many of them are wealthy merchants and landowners. Their horror of hurting life rules all their conduct. All the laws agree that not to hurt life is the highest virtue, and this view is carried out by them to the extremest point.

We went through the stream to the village, and found the government school. The master offered me the only chair and asked me if I would be good enough to draw out some of the things his boys had learned. They brought the *Amara* ("immortal"), a dictionary of Sanskrit nouns grouped with wondrous art in order of synonyms and showing their gender, in verse. It is a Jain work which could not be destroyed in the persecutions; the sea would not drown it.[70] Now it is the basis of all school teaching in languages dependent on Sanskrit. How the boys threw their energy into the tasks of clear enunciation of verses from memory! Then we had the *Padyasara,* a schoolbook of selections from Kannada poetry.[71] We read from that, "Beware of bad company," and "Who is a dalit?" Of course, one carefully guarded against any Christian reference on that neutral ground.

While we were inside the school, I was so absorbed in hearing the boys that I did not notice the verandahs were full of people listening. There was an audience waiting for us, and the priest of the temple among them. He was a noble-looking man, had graceful features and deep, thoughtful eyes. They fetched him a seat, and set it on one side of the verandah, and gave me the school chair on the other. They all listened intently to all we said. I could not help watching the expression on the priest's face. When we had finished, he said, "Our village is honored by your presence today, and we have listened with reverence to your words. You have spoken of sin and deliverance, but what about your own sins?"

---

69. There was some persecution of Buddhists in south India, where rivalries between Śaivite, Vaiṣṇavite, Jain, and Buddhist traditions at times became violent; but that Buddhism was driven from India by persecution is not accurate. (Cf. A. L. Basham, "There are other less reliable accounts of persecution, but it is certain that this was not the main cause of the disappearance of Buddhism from India" [2004, 267].)
70. The *Amarakosha* is generally dated to the sixth century AD and is described by Winternitz as "a dictionary of synonyms" (1985, 494). Winternitz further says that over fifty commentaries on the Amarakosha are known (ibid., 495). But the author, *Amarasiṁha,* is generally considered to have been Buddhist rather than Jain (Walker 1983, 1:345); and I can find no reference to a story of the sea not being able to drown this text.
71. A few copies of this obscure text are in libraries in the West.

"Would you please be good enough to tell me of them?" I said.

Solemnly fixing his piercing eyes upon me, he replied, as if his whole energy throbbed in his words, "Taking life is to us a sin for which there is no pardon. Taking life for food is more grievous still. But taking the life of the sacred cow for food is the abomination of all abominable sins."

I said, "Do you not think it would have been wise to ask first if I do commit that sin?"

"What," said he, "did ever a Briton live who did not eat beef?"

When I told him I did not eat beef or flesh, his wonderment grew until I said, "Ask my friend here; he knows my life."

He turned to John Mark, and when he had satisfied himself that I had really given up eating flesh food, it seemed as if there came into our talk a certain something I could feel but cannot tell. We talked till twilight, then left for our evening rest. Between the village and the stream I heard footsteps behind us, and found several men who had listened following. They said, "We should like to talk further if you can."

Gladly we asked them to go with us. We sat on a sandbank in the midst of the stream. The stars were so clear and seemed so brilliantly near that I could more than fancy heaven broods over earth. The men talked of their struggles toward the ideal. I told them of mine, and what I felt the Lord Jesus meant to me, what I felt He could be to them. The meal was forgotten for two or three hours, and I began to wonder if one had taken one real step toward crossing the gulf.

No Success

These are, I believe, fairly typical instances of our work during those days. I tried hard, as hard as strength would permit, to see what could be done by Kannadiga food and partly Kannadiga dress. So far as I know, I left nothing possible undone to reach the hearts of men, and to prepare myself to travel and preach, depending solely and alone upon what might be given one. The Lord's command to His disciples was ever sounding in my heart. I did not even then grasp all that was meant by "Go to your own alone, not to other nations."[72]

---

72. This reference to the words of Jesus in Matthew 10:5-6 is generally considered to be specific to that situation, and the later command of Matthew 28:18-20 seems to go against Robinson's point here.

They were among their own caste; I was being taught I was not, taught bitterly indeed. I walked barefoot always after the first few days, and kept myself wholly to the one purpose of avoiding everything that could offend.

When we were nearing Gubbi, I was so tired that I sat down in the springless cart to rest. John Mark smiled out the Kannada proverb, "The wrestler trained for twelve years, then threw a helpless old grandmother."[73]

---

73. I am unable to document this proverb. Robinson first wrote about this evangelistic tour in *The Harvest Field* in 1889, with some different details that make the article worth reading as a supplement to this chapter (Robinson 1889b; a link to access the article online is included with the reference information). The article also gives added details about the infirmities that followed this tour (mentioned in the first paragraph of the next chapter). The article closes with a promise of another article drawing conclusions, but this was never written, as Robinson's health broke the month the first article was published. This book, appearing twenty-three years later, fulfilled the promise made in 1889.

Chapter 3

Reflecting on Failure

Then I began to learn a little of my ignorance.

−Benjamin Robinson

"Baffled to fight better"[74]

DEPRESSION AND PAIN

When we had returned to Gubbi, I found that the seven weeks' strain had most severely tested nerves and digestive organs. There were lonely days, and nights of unnamable depression. Then came a crop of big, painful boils. One of the worst, in my left armpit, was so painful that I could only lie on my back with outstretched arm. I was too full of pain and exhaustion to read, and so had to face alone life's task and meaning. Why did I become a minister? Why did I leave the home work and come to Karnataka? Was my last venture absolutely necessary? Was it worth so much pain?

I could only feel after earnest search that in each case I had acted from a sincere conviction, to which I could not have been disobedient without inward wrong. I had then to face the results of my experiment in food and dress, and see how far it made one more efficient as a helper of men. Must it be continued? Could I hope to reach my aim of traveling without luggage of any sort?[75]

---

74. A phrase from the epilogue to Robert Browning's poem "Asolando" (Browning 1895, 1007).
75. During his recovery, Robinson wrote three articles which were published anonymously; see Robinson 1885a, b, and c. These are recommended reading, and links to the online versions are provided with the reference information. This comment about his tour must be noted:

> Little has been done, and that little has many a pang-causing remembrance of sin and failure, but all is filled with the mercy of Him who leadeth His own in life, though men call it the "Dream of a Shadow"; and as memory sketches the way of mercy's guidance, the weakened frame gathers strength, faith sinks down to and rests on His fidelity, until new strengthened from above the upward struggle is ease and joy unspeakable. So let me rest, and remember, and rise to the more reverent service of the Guide of human destiny. (Robinson 1885a, 6)

See note 8 on page xx for evidence that this is indeed Robinson writing.

A Crow among Peacocks

In Vrindāvan there was a sacred fig tree, where crows had nested and lived happily. There was a banyan tree near where peacocks lived. One of the crows, seeing the peacocks and crows together, thought to himself that the peacocks' caste was so much more excellent than his own that he picked up the peacocks' cast-off feathers, stuck them among his own, left his own family, and in his new guise lived among the peacocks as one of themselves for several days. One day his voice was heard, and the peacocks said, "This isn't a peacock; he has been deceiving us while living among us."

Then they all set upon him with beaks and spurs, till, sore wounded and shamed, he sought to get back again among his own family. The crows well understood why he left them, why he wished to return, and said to him, "You despised us, thinking you would honor yourself by trying to join others. Go to them now; there is no place for you here. Be off! We will not have you among us."

The Kannadiga moral is writ large: "Therefore whosoever, despising his own caste, seeks to pass himself off as belonging to another, he is good for nothing whatever; he is wholly gone to the bad."[76]

It was one thing to read the story. I was pointed out and laughed at as the crow. I had to learn what it meant through ridicule and shame.

In the mind of the Kannadiga people it is a self-evident truth that he who apes the customs and dress of another caste thereby confesses that caste is to him superior to his own.[77] That truth molds life. But one's own birth-status (*jāti*) cannot be altered. Our very makeup attests that. The attempt to appear as if belonging to another is gross, unworthy deceit—as senseless as useless. Inevitably the birth-constitution will out, the crow will caw, and the deceiver, cast out by both castes, goes to the bad. I could not have learned the inwardness of the story without making the experiment. How much it cost me! That must be learned and owned when we talk of "native dress."

---

76. I have not been able to locate this folktale in the various collections and analyses of Indian folktales, but note a YouTube version of the story for children at https://www.youtube.com/watch?v=hWigMiL3zzE.
77. Even with the impact of modernity, there remain today dress codes distinctive to certain caste groups; particularly, Brāhmans refuse to wear what is distinctive of other castes. Some of the distinctions are too minute for an untrained eye to even notice, such as the way something is worn rather than just what is worn.

A Wesleyan Hindu

I had a dear Brāhman friend. He called himself a Wesleyan Hindu. He had been trained in our high school, deeply admired his teachers, and reverenced our Lord Jesus sincerely. "I cannot become a Christian," he would say. There were some things in our system he could not accept, and many in his ancestral faith that he could not leave; but he was one of the noblest, truest men.

When a little strength returned and pain lessened, I wrote to him, telling him what I had done, my purpose and my hope. He wrote back, "Caste is birth. Whatever you do, you cannot alter it. However you dress or eat, you will be and will be known as an Englishman. Your motives in change of dress would be misunderstood and misconstrued."

I had asked him to tell me frankly; I believe he did. Years of thought have taught me how true and sane his judgment was.

Concluding against Indian Dress

Soon after I resumed duties [in my educational work], I was at Kunigal, and rode out a few miles to call on the headman at Bidinagiri [Bidanagere]. He was taught in our day school, gave up the worship of material forms, and set up in front of his house carved stones of witness that God is One, that idolatry is vain, and that there is but one Savior. He could not become a Christian outwardly by baptism. He was a Sudra, respected—one might almost say revered—by all who knew him, for his real worth.

When he saw me, he said solemnly and earnestly, "I am right glad to see you in your own proper dress. I hope you will never change it again."

I told him my purpose in doing as I had done. I cannot tell how he spoke. It was as if I were sitting at the feet of a teacher, whose words and personality filled me with awe, as he said, "Don't you perceive, sir, that if you adopt the dress of these idolaters, they will say, 'You ought to adopt our worship, too'?"

That thought had never come to me. Its force in its bearing upon my whole life-work made me tremble.[78]

---

78. This illustrates the conundrum of contextualization. Adopting the ways of the "other" might communicate that the "other" is right, but *not* adopting the ways of the "other" gives the impression that a foreign religion and way of life is being promoted. The latter is nowadays generally recognized as the more serious and fundamental error; thus the promotion of contextual expressions of faith despite the risks involved.

The judgment of friends supported the ridicule of others. Both together confirmed the conviction ripening within that the change of dress could not help, but must hinder, me as a minister of Christ among the Kannadiga people. As to flesh food, the feeling that to eat it was an outrage upon the most sacred conviction of the great majority of people around me was so strong and overwhelming within me that I determined not to eat beef or pork, and to abstain from all other meat as far as health and courtesy to others would allow. Though here one feared possible misconstruction. In Sanskrit stories, when old tigers, cats, and herons can no longer easily get prey, they are made to feign penitence for having eaten flesh, and to use that as a device for obtaining new opportunity.

The Cat and the Vulture

A cat wished to eat some young birds. Seeing an old blind vulture who lived on the charity of other birds, the cat spoke to him. "Who are you?" said the vulture.

"A cat."

"Get thee hence, wicked animal!"

"What! Is a cat to be punished or praised simply because he is a cat? Only when you know his conduct thoroughly can you justly decide whether he deserves praise or blame."

"What is your method of life?" said the vulture.

"I bathe daily, I never eat flesh, I am a bachelor-student. Let me share the hollow of your tree. For it is written:

> 'The good are gracious to the lowest animals,
>
> Does the moon withhold her light from the dalit's hut?'"[79]

"Ah! But cats have a taste for flesh, and young birds live above."

The cat touched her two ears and the ground in solemn oath, and swore it read the divine laws and had forsaken all such evil practices. But after it had gained the vulture's hollow tree as its home, it ate the young birds on the sly. When the parent birds began to inquire who ate their nestlings, the cat slunk off, and they killed the vulture![80]

---

79. I have been unable to trace this proverb.
80. The vulture and cat story is found in the Hitopadesha; http://mocomi.com/hitopadesha-the-story-of-the-vulture-the-cat-and-the-birds/.

That principle meets one always, and our whole method of work is said to be guileful stratagem to lead men away from caste rather by fraud than attempt it by force.[81] Thus pondering, I felt that abstinence from flesh food was my only course.

Caste and Custom

"Native" is used ordinarily as the result of a hasty, if not ignorant, generalization. All non-Europeans in India are "natives." All are treated as one homogeneous whole, and as if, therefore, it were simplicity itself to adopt native dress. The deep, ineffaceable distinctions are only seen and felt after such a test as I had made. Which native dress should I wear? I could not wear all even of those worn in Karnataka; and I learned that Karnataka is but a small province of India, which has many more differences.

"Adopt native food and manner" had been urged upon me from all motives and quarters. I was told it would promote health, it would help to make one's work more effective, and was the only means of saving missionary work from failure.[82] Which caste custom was I to adopt? I could not adopt them all. Some I dared not for the sake of manhood. I tried in the most careful way possible to see how one form of food affected health, and for me it caused an illness which has brought years of pain.

I have thought through the results of those months of struggle, and after the most careful scrutiny possible to me, something like the following outline seems clear: "Caste," as we call it from the Portuguese *casta* (breed or race), is in Karnataka *jāti* (i.e., birth, family, tribe). Birth determines caste; caste is birth. Constitution, condition, life-function, follow from that. No one can alter his birth; birth is destiny, divine and sacred—the prearranged reward or punishment of past deeds. Food is a family sacrifice; birth alone gives right there. Caste customs are as necessary and inevitable to each caste as life function is to each family of animals.

---

81. The accusation of duplicity is still raised in response to contextualization, for example by Sita Ram Goel:

    The solution to the problem, as the Board of Management sees it, is to invent spurious labels which can hoodwink Hindus into believing that a brand new product is being brought to them. That is what Christian theologians, historians, sociologists, artists and musicians are working at today. (2009, 7)

    There must be the utmost integrity to demonstrate that this is not the case, and priority in these matters must rest with insiders to the traditions rather than with outside cross-cultural workers.

82. This hyperbolic statement is in conflict with earlier statements that no one supported Robinson in his experiment. Clearly he was hearing strong opinions from both sides, related to the controversy on this issue mentioned in the Introduction (pg. xxi) and surveyed in appendix 3.

If I attempt to adopt any other caste custom than that of my birth, it means I despise my own and acknowledge the other as superior; but I only deceive myself. I am what I was born. If I could really adopt the customs of any caste and be acknowledged by that caste as truly belonging to its family, it would mean that I brought myself into the sectional antagonisms of castes, which would make the universal purpose of God's love in Christ for all men as brothers impossible.[83]

Personal Unworthiness

Those convictions made one outward method of work impossible to me, but the purpose and aim of that method, the aim of my life, was still beyond. How could I bring the love of Christ as the law of life into the source of other men's motives? Rather, how could Christ himself do it in and through me? My attempt to reach others turned in upon myself. How far was I inwardly, spiritually equipped for such a task? The sense of unworthiness even to bear the name of Christ grew. It seemed as if all the years of discipleship had but made Him say of me, "You know not what manner of spirit you are of." "Do not mind the things of men, but of God."[84]

As I prayed for insight, humility, and teachableness to learn of Christ, there came with clear commanding force the conviction that I must aim at the moral motives of men, their new creation in the Spirit of Jesus. To attempt to change outward conditions and forms first, and still leave men what they were before in their self-centeredness, was of little avail. What men are in the moral quality of the self, that counts. I could not, however much I wished, bridge over the chasms of birth, but all the more deeply was the need of spiritual re-birth pressed into me.

---

83. This comment reveals Robinson's inability to transcend the standard understanding of caste in his time. The goal of transcending caste by avoiding its "sectional antagonisms" is not even possible; those who attempt such avoidance only become yet another caste! The alternative perspective is that the gospel must take root among all peoples, which means among all languages and castes and tribes. The universality that Robinson appropriately brings into focus does not suggest uniformity but radical adaptability. The universal gospel when planted in higher-caste Hindu society will bring transformations in an organic way, quite different in method and result from attempts to force change from outside. Caste has always been changing, and has changed drastically from what Robinson described. It is doubtful that the association of caste and occupation was ever as absolute as Robinson suggested; he stated the theory, but there were always significant exceptions. Exceptions to the "caste determines occupation" idea have almost become the rule in twenty-first century modernity.
84. These are words of Jesus found in Luke 9:55 (King James Version) and Mark 8:33.

The Lord's own method, life touching life to divine issues, began to grow plain; I was impelled to try to follow Him in that. How high, how hard, it seemed! I must be what I wished others to become. It was hard to bear ridicule, shame, and pain. But what must it mean to become the organ of Christ through which He alone should act—act with the highest force He could communicate to His instrument? I trembled at my calling, but I dared not shrink from it. I sought grace to try again.

Then I began to learn a little of my ignorance. Had I learned more inwardly the thought of the people, in their best books and in the lives of the best men, I should have seen that some of the necessary data for solving the life-problem before me were not yet mine. Yet I do not know how I could have reached the point from which I could gain the necessary insight if I had not made that experiment. How little I really knew of their inward thought, its heights and depths! My ignorance of their sacred scriptures appalled me. I was most deeply ashamed that I had ever attempted to teach. I could no longer be content with secondhand presentations of their thought. I was impelled by a force I could not resist to set myself to learn as much as I could of their scriptures in the original,[85] so that the spirit and genius of it might be grasped. Putting myself into the spiritual position of the people, I would thus teach them the life of Christ's love.

The Need to Learn

Once I went with a missionary to a village as he was going to preach. There was in the village a Brāhman student who had just come home from the great school at Sringeri, the seat of their great high priest.[86] He is called the *jagadguru*, the world-spiritual-director of the Smārta Brāhmans. The student and the missionary began talking of religion; and the conversation, as always, soon centered in the unbeginning past, deeds done in which determine the present.

"Is it fair," said the missionary, "for God to reward or punish us in this life for deeds done in a past life of which we have no memory?" "Were you ever an infant?" "Yes, of course." "Have you any memory of your infancy?" "No."

---

85. This represents the error of assuming the centrality of texts to Hindu traditions. Arvind Sharma dates a great change in the field of Hindu studies to "after the 1960s, when a new body, and even new generation, of scholars began to combine textual work with at least a stay in the field, if not fieldwork in the anthropological sense" (Sharma 2003, x). The lived realities of all faith traditions are different than their scriptural statements, and this is emphatically the case in regard to Hindu traditions.
86. Sringeri has a famous *matha* ["monastery"] founded by the great philosopher Sankara; see http://www.sringeri.net/history for traditions related to this.

"Yet you must admit that period of which you have no memory has been the most fruitful." "Yes, but though I have no memory of infancy, I have friends who knew me as a baby; and their witness, together with what I have seen of children, certifies to me that I was an infant. What is witness to that unbeginning past?"

The Brāhman hissed out two words, "*Śastrave sakshi*" ("The scripture itself is witness"). I can see and hear him now. His training made itself felt in every thought, in every tone. The whole energy of the man was uttered in those two words.

In that hour I was convinced that missionary work in India means the contact and conflict of the Sanskrit and Christian scriptures—the Veda and the Bible. Each is the flower and fruit of a nation's spirit and genius. Who yet knows, who can tell, all the differences in their presuppositions, their goal, their discipline? Whatever may be the forms of action and interaction of the faiths arising out of and nourished by those scripture sources, all must prepare for and center in that great conflict. Its issues for our race, for the millions of men professing such varied faiths from those sources, who can tell? As we sat in the verandah, I vowed that I would try to learn the meaning and spirit of that "scripture-witness," so that I might feel with the men to whom I would teach Jesus. I must learn the scripture itself if it were possible; I could not be content with what others said about it.

During those three years, whatever the outer form of duty, I worked hard at the prescribed Kannada examinations—in the study of books, of spoken words, and of the underlying thought, as far as I could. It was no easy task.[87] At first there was a perpetual mental translation from English into Kannada. I was urged on to aim at thinking, dreaming Kannada. It must become the innermost part of my very self, before I could hope to make it the medium of persuading men.

---

87. Robinson 1885b contains deeper reflections on language and culture learning, a highly recommended paper for further understanding Benjamin Robinson.

When I asked my teacher for the meaning of some terms in the beginning of Kannada grammar, he said "that must be learned in Sanskrit." He gave the same reply when asked for the derivation and makeup of words. Therefore, in my first year I learned the Sanskrit characters, and continued that study in addition to Kannada.[88] Time and further study made the necessity of Sanskrit as the key to all religious thought to me imperative.

One of our Kannadiga ministers said to me, "If we could only learn enough Sanskrit to cope with Brāhmans on equal terms, how it would help us in our preaching!" Every step made me feel that one must live oneself into the very spirit of the people. Their religious thought came from the Sanskrit; I must learn that, and the thought of the people too.

---

88. Robinson's three annual language exams are noted in the archival record. Related to his first-year exam, the report states that "Altogether the examination gave us great satisfaction & we think that Mr. Robinson gives promise of attaining high excellence in the knowledge & use of the Kannarese language" (UTC, "Minutes of the Mysore District Meeting Begun in Bangalore January 2, 1884," in Synod Minutes 1877-1897, C37/B, MMS 21, 286). The report on his third and final exam gives an indication of the rigor involved: "He was also examined orally. His pronunciation and reading were very good. But the examination showed that while careful and laborious attention had been given to grammatical forms, less care had been devoted to the higher branches of syntax & lexicography" (UTC, "Minutes of the Mysore District Meeting Held in Bangalore Jan 4th 1886," in Synod Minutes 1877-1897, C37/B, MMS 21, 346).

Chapter 4

Learning

I was impelled by that experience to search further into the spirit of their scripture . . .

–Benjamin Robinson

Learning went to the Brāhman and said, "I am thy Treasure, guard me."
—Manu. 2.114[89]

A NEW HOME

The Rājah of Sakrayapatna [Sakharayapatna] had two daughters. He gave one town to each upon marriage. The one is "town of the elder daughter," Hiremagalur; the other, "town of the younger daughter," Chikkamagalur. At Hiremagalur there is a stone pillar, carved as ascending flame. There a famous king made a snake-sacrifice; and it is firmly believed that if anyone bitten by a cobra comes to the pillar, then drinks of the holy well nearby, and walks round it in prayer three times, he will be saved from the poison. In a small temple there is a stone representing the axe of the Brāhman hero, Parasu Rāma, who with his axe cleared the earth of the kingly caste twenty-one times.[90] There one stands on the border of the holy land of the Brāhmans. The town of the younger daughter has outgrown that of the elder, is the head of a district, and is of importance in the coffee growth and trade.

---

89. The 1912 edition of this book contains an error here, referring to Manu. 2.14. The correct reference, *Manusmriti* or *Mānava Dharmaśāstra* or *The Laws of Manu* 2.114, has been provided (see Olivelle 2006, 100). Olivelle translates "Vedic knowledge" rather than "learning," but the Sanskrit text (ibid., 423) says merely *vidhyā*, knowledge or learning.
90. Parasurama, whose name means "Ram of the Axe," is considered the sixth of ten avataras of Vishnu. His father was murdered by Kshatriyas (the kingly caste) in a long-running dispute. Walker summarizes,
    that while his father's body was being cremated he took a solemn oath before the gods that he would exterminate the whole race of the accursed Kshatriyas. He first massacred the sons of Kartavirya, and then embarked upon his famous expeditions. "Thrice seven times" did he clear the earth of the Kshatriya clans, filling with their blood the great lakes of Samanta-panchaka and Kurukshetra (1983, 2:190.)

My house at Chikmagalur[91] was built of mud, native tiles, no ceiling nor glass, a mud floor—which was duly cleansed with *sagani* (cow dung), the precious sin-destroying cleanser. At first it was disagreeable, but one grew to feel it might be pure. Rats would run up my bedposts; a snake would draw a frog into its hole under the door. But green grass—not English turf, but nearest like it of any I saw in Karnataka—grew there in the rains. The highest peak of the Chandra Drona Mountains overlooked the town; thence had been brought a perennial stream of water. By the side of the house was a plot of rank grass, which spade work turned into a garden, in which water, soil, and climate helped to grow the best English vegetables I grew in Karnataka, and sweet potatoes as big as a forearm. My garden is always to me a symbol of my life-work. I hoped that garden might thrive there.

As soon as the prescribed language tests were passed, I set myself to the study of ancient Kannada and Sanskrit. To do that I religiously continued the method of my Gubbi life. I rose at 4 A.M., and spent two hours in prayers and study. At 6 A.M. I had a light meal of plantains, bread, and water. Then I visited a village to preach or examine a school. At 10 A.M. I was back for breakfast, after which came half-an-hour's rest. From 12 to 3 I read with my *munshi* [language teacher].[92] Private study followed until 5. Then I worked an hour in the garden, or went to bazaar preaching, or received Kannadiga friends. I dined, as convenient, at any time after 7:30, and retired to rest at 10 P.M.

The Inner Being

In ancient Kannada study I came upon a passage where a king, receiving his crown, said he would govern according to *manassākshi* (i.e., "the witness of the internal sense"). That was the very word European missionaries used for "conscience." It was held that they had coined it, as there was no word for conscience in Sanskrit or Kannada. It startled me to find the word used more than a thousand years before, in a sense that certainly was near to the Christian sense. At every point one felt the need of an appeal to the inner man.[93]

---

91. Archival references to Robinson's time in Chikmagalur are not particularly clear. See notes 21, 22, and 24 on pages xxx-xxxi for the details.
92. *The Harvest Field* for October 1885 contains an anonymous paper entitled "My Munshi" that is most likely written by Robinson. This is recommended for understanding more about the language-learning process and is available online (see under References Cited, Robinson 1885d).
93. An example of Robinson attempting such an appeal is present in his story told in Robinson 1885e, 140 and on page 49 of this book.

Then in the Sanskrit Dharma Shāstra (i.e., Sacred Law Book) I came upon the verse, "Verily the wicked think, 'No one sees us,' but the gods watch them and their inner man." There is a story in the Mahābhārata telling how a king was hunting near a famous hermitage. The hermit was absent, but his adopted daughter gave the king their best hospitality. The king married her there, promised to fetch her to his palace, and said that her son should succeed him on his throne. He did not fulfill his promise. When her son was thirteen years old, the hermit bade her go to the Rājah with the lad, and claim his promise. The king denied all knowledge of her. Then she said, "The wicked, when he sins, thinks, 'I am all alone, no one sees'; but the sun and moon see, the heavenly gods see, and the inward personality sees."[94]

Those thoughts prompted my first Kannada booklet. I placed that thought first from their own sacred scriptures, and tried to appeal to the inner man in the spirit of the Sacred Law Book, which says, "Despise not, then, (your) own self, the highest witness of men."[95]

When the tract was submitted for printing, it was said, "A Kannadiga man might read this and worship all the more fervently in the next idol temple to which he came." That was intended as condemnation, I believe. I could not but feel if a man were moved to more fervent worship in the best way he knew, because of the inner self-witness to sin, that was the first step toward betterment.

The tract was eventually printed, and a missionary friend said years afterwards it was eagerly read by literary Brāhmans. That set me thinking more deeply. How easy it is to claim to coin a word when you are ignorant of an ancient literature! How much care is needed if what we deem an exact equivalent of one of our concepts is not expressed in another in one word, lest we should hastily conclude that the thing is unknown. I was impelled by that experience to search further into the spirit of their scripture, that I might reach the inner personality of every man.

---

94. This is a very brief summary of the famous story of Shakuntala. The moral of the story that Robinson quotes in introducing and closing his account is translated this way by van Buitenen (Shakuntala is speaking):

> A man who has done wrong thinks, 'Nobody knows me.' But the Gods know him, and his own inner soul. Sun and Moon, Wind and Fire, Heaven, Earth and Water, and his heart and Yama, and Day and Night, and both the Twilights, and the Law all know the doings of each man. (MBh. 1.68.25-29; van Buitenen 1973, 1:166).

95. I have been unable to trace this reference.

The Golden Rule

The study of that year strengthened what had been growing within me all along. "Whatsoever ye would that men should do unto you, even so do ye also unto them," must determine one's whole inner attitude toward the people, their scriptures, and their religion.[96] I began to feel that denouncing the worst things in people, and holding up their sacred things to ridicule, were wholly contradictory to the spirit and word of our Lord. I could not hold up the worst debasement of idolatry, so unspeakably sensual, and whatever is worst in Kannadiga life, and claim that it was all the result of their religion, which was, therefore, bad, and must be forsaken; then, on the other side, hold up a purely ideal form of the Christian religion, and compare the ideal of one side with the actual life of the other. I do not judge that method, but I could not follow it myself.

If a Brāhman came to England and proclaimed that our drunkenness, our social evils, our political methods, and much that we deplore in our national life was the direct outcome of our religion, and a sure sign of its utter badness, I should demur, and demand that it must first be considered how far they were results necessarily growing out of our religion, and so indicating its moral quality. I felt the Lord's rule claimed that I should put myself in the Kannadiga men's place, and see what they thought. I soon found that they resented the suggestion of evil practices being the inevitable outgrowth of their religion, as energetically as I should if the Brāhman had made the charge to me about Christianity. If the Brāhman held up an ideal interpretation of the Vedic faith as the only faith for man, and condemned our actual life from the standpoint of his ideal, I should ask, "Is that ideal real? Is yours the only interpretation of your scripture, or are there differences deep and wide among yourselves?"

The Kannadiga Brāhman who has been taught English judges Christians thus—sometimes captiously, sometimes carefully and reverently. They hold that there are few, if any, true followers of Jesus now. The meekness of our Savior has appealed to their inner self, and their reverence for Him is only equaled by their perception of the difference between His New Testament portraiture and European Christians—yes, European missionaries. They see the differences between Christians that have no communion with each other, each claiming to be the only true faith, the only true way of salvation, and they ask, "Which Christian religion must we accept?"

---

96. This statement of Jesus, often called the Golden Rule, is from Matthew 7:12; Robinson is certainly right to apply this thought to interreligious interaction.

I could but feel one must learn more and more inwardly what the best, confessedly so among themselves, really amounted to, in ideal and aim. How much there is of kinship between that and our Lord's ideal and life gradually grew upon me with fuller study. I could then fairly and with good conscience compare our failure—mine, not theirs only—in the presence of that ideal. Our deep need for inward help then became plain. It was above question that the meek goodness of our Lord was the life commanded by the highest ethical standard. From that position I could the more fervently and faithfully confess my faith in Him as leading unworthy me into His own fellowship. There was no other course for me than to learn the best in all their thought, compare the worst with that, and thence appeal to the inward need of forgiveness, of saving grace to help a man against himself, and lead him to become what he wished to be.

Religiosity

Sacrificial thought and practice ruled the life of ancient Brāhmans, but the teaching of Gautama [Buddha] concerning the sanctity of life, perhaps also the feeling of Brāhmans themselves, caused animal sacrifices to cease among them almost absolutely. Sacrifice now is mental and symbolical, though every meal is still a sacrifice.[97] It impressed me greatly to learn that this change of attitude toward sacrifice should have gone on in India just before our Lord's death caused the abolition of animal sacrifices. All the more deeply I thought of what His sacrifice of Himself meant. "He bore our sins in His own body on the tree."[98] What could that mean if it did not mean that the Sinless One counted our sins as His own not personally, but in that inward unity of manhood which made Him all He is to us?

The dreadful debasement of life, especially in the case of the women who were dedicated to the temple service of Karnataka, the exemption of temple sculpture from the penal code, the awful miasma of degrading superstition which poisoned men and paralyzed them—these and many forms of unnamable evil entered into one with feeling words do not know. But the women devoted to the gods from before birth were women—children of our Father, our sisters—mine; and the pain of their sin burdened, almost crushed, me. The men who confessed to me they could not help such and such sins were men. The priests of Mari, the goddess of lust, blood, and death[99]—I saw

---

97. Food is still considered a sacrifice, particularly on special occasions.
98. 1 Peter 2:24.
99. *Mari* is more widely known as *Mariamma* (Mother Mari), the great mother goddess of south India once known as goddess of smallpox.

them at their worship, and felt a little of what their life meant. I saw men run barefoot through hottest fires; men worship the unseen powers with fire, and call them with their bells.

All the tragedy of it grew upon me. Were all these men my brothers? Yes, if Christ is the Savior of all. I began to feel their sin as the sin of my own flesh and blood, to confess it with shame and confusion of face, to feel my own weakness, and pray for saving grace for us all.

Two Srivaishnava Brāhmans often came to my little hut in Chikmagalur. One of them had been trained in one of our high schools. We talked of books and religion. The student of our school said, "One of your missionaries taught us in school that Jesus Christ is the very essence of God," and added, "Therefore, God must be rubbish."

At first I could not see his thought at all; but after I had considered a moment, it was clear. The mental process was, I thought, something like this: "Essence of God? Yes; essence is the life-sap of a tree, then the vital quality of anything which, if taken away, leaves the rest sapless, worthless."

Once he brought to see me a learned man, a poet, who was staying with him for some days. My friend was a coffee planter. The poet had written a poem on coffee—*kapi*, as it is called there. He derived the word from a Sanskrit verb "to drink." I suggested the word was derived from a foreign tongue, but he said it must be so treated when once the word was used in their poetry. Then the poem extolled the virtues of coffee, and accounted for it thus. There was a lady attendant in Vishnu's heaven, *Vaikuntha,* of whom Vishnu was very fond because of her beauty and devotion. Then she offended the god, and he condemned her to earth; but for the sake of her former devotion she was to become the beautiful tree which bears the refreshing berry.

The next time my friend came, he told me the poet while there had written some erotic verses, and added with energy, "You blame us for our tendencies, but those verses soothed my soul. I cannot help it; it is in our very blood."

When one of the elder ladies of his house died, I condoled with him. He told me how happily she died. She could see Vishnu's heaven in all its glory and beauty, and Vishnu's attendants were there with smiling faces to carry her that she might prostrate herself at his feet.

One day he said to me, "Will you tell us frankly what is your relation to the British government?"

"What exactly do you mean?"

"Are you in any sense agents of the British government? With us religion is an affair of state, and the Rājah must see that it is strong. Is your work intended really to strengthen British rule in India?"

When I said our only relation to the British government was that of loyal subjects, and that we were in no sense, paid or otherwise, agents of the crown, he seemed incredulous. We talked long about it; I believe he accepted my word, and yet found it difficult to believe there was nothing behind.

A Child Dies in Christ

I went to the girls' school regularly for the scripture lessons. The Gospels there became Eastern books to me. I tried to let the Eastern local coloring of our Lord's words affect the children and myself.

After one of the girls died, I went to visit her father. He was sitting in his shop. Tears filled his eyes as I said, "Your heart must be very sore."

"Yes, my heart is very sore; but I wanted to see you, to tell you my Kamala did not speak about our god and our bliss beyond when she was ill; she was always talking about the things you taught her out of your book, about your Jesus, Lord and Savior. She kept on repeating your prayer to 'Our Father.' And when she died, she said she was going to Jesus."

The Hills of Western Karnataka

I spent several weeks visiting the coffee planters on their estates, and teaching in the villages as well. The Malnad (i.e., rain country) in the west of Karnataka is holy ground to Brāhmans. By titanic force one of the sons of Brahmā, in pride and rage, hurled the earth into the sea. Vishnu took the form of a boar, whose eyes were the sun and moon. His tusks were *tunga* (uplifted) and *bhadra* (strong). When by the might of his tusks he had heaved up the earth from the sea, he rested from his labor on the "Boar Mountain." As the perspiration trickled down his tunga tusk it formed the source of the Tunga River; and [the perspiration] that [trickled down his] bhadra [tusk] formed the source of the Bhadra. The two streams rise together on the Boar Mountain, separate, flow through valleys among the Chandra Drona group of mountains, and join to form the Tunga Bhadra, eight miles east of Shimoga.[100]

---

100. Wikipedia has a long article on the Tungabhadra River, but without reference to this myth (https://en.wikipedia.org/wiki/Tungabhadra_River).

The valleys through which they flow, crowned by massive mountains, are of wondrous beauty. Trees bear brilliant flowers; their new budding leaves equal flowers in beauty of tone. The frankincense trees are as graceful as they are fragrant. Bamboos, looking like majestic ferns, have fronds many yards high. Orchids thrive in tree forks and branches. In the valleys grow rice, sugar, and the choicest areca nut palms. On the mountain slopes, under the shade of selected giant trees, Mysore coffee blooms into fruit. Tree ferns, canes, and ferns down to the finest forms grow under trees or in damp rocks. The river sometimes broadens out like a lake and reflects heaven and all around with tender grace, then will rush through rocky gorges, or seemingly play through lovely cascades.

The banks of these streams were chosen by the ancient sages for the sites of their hermitages, where they could ponder the eternal divine. The earliest parts of the "science-section" of the Vedas are called "forest-studies."[101] When the Brāhman teacher had performed his household duties, and his sons could take charge of his home, he retired to the forest to prepare to rejoin the source of life. To such studies we owe the spirit of life. To such studies we owe the spirit of the Upanishads, which molds thought in India today powerfully, and is spreading westward. Streams, hills are sacred to the memory of such thinkers still. As you travel there the spirit of the mighty forests and the rivers wins to deep thought, reverence, and worship. There the sages questioned into the deepest depths of self within, and to the furthest bound of thought above, around.

Sacred Places

At Tirthahalli the river has worn the rocky bed into strange forms. In the center is the *tirtha* (i.e., holy bathing place). A passage has been worn under a rock, part of which is left like a bridge, the water gurgling through up the other side. Whoever bathes there, and passes under the rock, emerges free from every stain. I wondered how it could be done alive. Rāma the axe-bearer was commended by his father to avenge his honor on his wife, who had dishonored him. Obedience to father and reverence for mother were binding duties. He obeyed his father, but the stain of vengeance on his mother clung to his inner man. After all possible expiation and visiting in penance every holy place, a stain of sin as big as a mustard seed could not be cleansed away, until he passed under this *tirtha*. Then he was wholly pure.[102]

---

101. Robinson's "science-section" clearly refers to the *jñānakanda* of the Vedas (the Aranyakas and Upanishads), a debatable translation, as "knowledge section" would be more accurate; his "forest-studies" refers to the Aranyakas, a much more acceptable translation.
102. There is a version of this myth on the internet, but the stain is not in Parshuram's inner man but on his axe (https://kalyangeetha.wordpress.com/2018/04/27/map-of-sri-rama-temples-2000/).

Agastya was the great sage who is revered as the father of learning in the south.[103] His name and wondrous power of devotion haunts Kalasa and the mountains round. There is a temple there, said to have been built to atone for the sin of taking life in the chase. There I saw a student chanting his Sanskrit lesson over and over in the temple porch. I asked if he would be good enough to tell me the meaning, and he said, "The meaning is not yet given."

From the temple gate, the main street of the old city was clear—mounds of ruin on each side covered with grass. A few Brāhman houses were there still. I was asked to sit down in the verandah of one. The Brāhman was, I think, glad to receive a Gospel in Sanskrit, but said, "Who can teach me its meaning? I want a spiritual guide to teach me truly."

I had to leave after some time, wishing true spiritual guides could be raised up and sent to such.

But Sringeri is the holiest spot of all.[104] A sage lived there whose mighty devotion enabled him to reduce his foes to ashes by his flashing eyes. He caused a son, Rishya Sringa (i.e., the deer-horned sage), to be born apart from human aid. The lad grew to early manhood without seeing a woman. The kingdom of Anga suffered sore from drought and famine. The sages said that Rishya Sringa must be brought from his father's hermitage and marry the king's adopted daughter; but they feared his father's eyes. The loveliest maidens were sent, disguised as hermits, to decoy him away. In the father's absence they fascinated the youth, until he joined them at their hermitage, which was a raft on the river. He was borne away willingly in their company. He married the king's daughter, and afterward he performed the sacrifice which caused the birth of Rāma, the incarnation of Vishnu, as the ideal king. Rāma himself visited there during his exile, and the mountain is pointed out where he met Hanuman, the monkey-god, who helped to save Rāma's wife from Rāvana.[105]

Twelve hundred years ago Sankarāchārya formulated the *advaita*—"non-dual"—system of religious thought, which has since ruled all the thought

---

103. Cf. Walker, "Agastya is 'lord of the southern region' of Bharat, and his name is highly venerated in south India. Traditionally, he was the first teacher to bring the light of science and literature to the Dravidian peoples and was said to be the originator of Tamil grammar" (1983, 1:11). There are many myths about Agastya on a Wikipedia page about him (https://en.wikipedia.org/wiki/Agastya).
104. See note 86 on page 29.
105. A version of this story is recounted on the Sringeri temple website at http://www.sringeri.net/history/sage-rishyashringa.

of Smārta Brāhmans and deeply affected the systems that differ from it. The questioning of the sages in the Upanishads varied much in scope and quality. It seems hard to make all cohere in one consistent whole. Thence Sākya Muni, the Buddha, had drawn his thought which so deeply questioned the roots of thinking.[106] His followers were persecuted, and his form of religious thought was banished from his home.[107] Still, it left its mark on the thinking of the Brāhmans.

There are hints of earlier attempts to systematize the thought of the ancient scriptures. The *Brahma Sutras* are one of the most noteworthy efforts to form Brāhmanic thought in the compressed mnemonic phrases which they perfected. Sankara, by his commentary on those Sutras and on the Upanishads, defined the non-dualist interpretation of the Vedas and of life, and defended it against all others. As a record of thinking it amazes one the more one studies it. There our axioms are questioned, our certainties are illusion. But when the spreading influence of that system of thought touches us more nearly, and when we have learned enough to feel its force in India, we shall find that conflict with it will compel the reconsideration of all our own schemes and systems.

Sankara founded the seat of the "world's spiritual-director" at Sringeri. For twelve hundred years there has been an unbroken succession of them, all buried—not burned, as other Brāhmans—at Sringeri.[108] They are chosen as children by certain marks, which divinely signify their destiny. I could not look at Sringeri unmoved. The country had its charm, but the history of so many life-molding forces which have centered there filled me with reverent awe.

The forests, mountains, valleys, and rivers seemed somehow to become part of myself. I could but worship there, though sometimes the squalor of man contrasted strangely with the splendor around. I do not know if the spirit of the forest did it, but it was as if one began to feel something of the inwardness of the Brāhman's feeling for the Veda. It is the most sacred family heritage.

---

106. The relationship of Buddha and Buddhist thought to the Upanishads is not so simple and clear as stated here by Robinson. Note the brief summary in De Bary's *Sources of Indian Tradition*, which refers to "the bewildering variety of doctrines which were canvassed by the ascetic groups of the time" (1958, 1:39).
107. See note 69 on page 19.
108. On burial rather than cremation for holy men, see Klostermaier: "Hindus usually burn their dead, except in times of great disasters. Some sects like the Viraśaivas [Lingāyats] practice burial. Also small children and *samnyasis* are buried" (1994, 189).

The Brāhman youth is twice born from the Veda and for its sake.[109] For long periods it would seem to have been handed down from teacher to disciples, tested and found worthy. Divine powers were stored in its truth. That truth must not be taught to an unworthy, unauthorized person, as men do not sow good seed in salt soil. Even if a teacher were in dire distress, and teaching the Veda to the unworthy would save him from death, he must prefer to die and let his knowledge burn with his body.

The Veda is the highest characteristic expression of the Hindu genius and spirit. It is their very own—the spirit and life of their blood. Hence comes their wonder at our pressing our scripture on every one, and they will sometimes say, "Can that be good which needs so much pressing?"

Illness Again

On my way home from one of my journeys in the holy land of the Brāhmans, I halted at a damp, cheerless rest-house. After the moist heat of the day, it repelled one. The terrible ache in every part of the body foretold coming malaria.[110] After a sleepless night, with great difficulty I rode to a drier resting place. Then the malaria began, all one's frame shaking with cold, though the thermometer stood at about 90 degrees. Burning heat followed, then perspiration, till I collapsed in utter weakness.

Home was dear and far then. A Scottish friend, after my return, said, "Very sorry you have been ill; fear you did too much."

---

109. This is a rather odd statement; Brāhman boys have their second birth in the Upanayana ceremony, which traditionally begins the process of learning the Vedas. Most Brāhmans today do not learn the Vedas, and many do not wear the sacred thread with which they are invested during the Upanayana ceremony.
110. Robinson uses the word *ague*. This is Robinson's second health crisis and it does not seem to be directly related to his embracing of an Indian lifestyle, or to overwork.

Chapter 5

Dialog with Brāhmans

The old man within me prompted retort,
but I tried to learn deeper meekness.

–Benjamin Robinson

"'Tis a life-long toil till our lump be leaven,
The better! What's come to perfection perishes."[111]

ANOTHER RELOCATION

A sage was seeking a site for his hermitage. On the bank of the Tunga he found a spot where the buds of herbs for his simple food were sweet and tender. He called it *shi mogge* (sweet budding herbs). We call it Shimoga.[112]

Shimoga Circuit was then about six thousand square miles in area. There were one and a quarter millions of non-Christian people and one Protestant European missionary. If the missionary and his Kannadiga helpers had had nothing to do but teach, and could secure on an average an audience of twenty-five persons daily, it would have taken thirteen years for every person in that area to hear about Christ once.

On the west were the noble, wide-spreading forests of the Ghats, drenched with rain; ninety miles eastward was Chitaldrug [Chitradurga], the driest place in the province. During the rains, everything grew moldy. When the hot season began, every bit of wood in the bungalow began to crack. The very name of Shimoga was dreaded for fever by the plains country people. All that is mortal of two missionaries' wives lies in its cemetery.

---

111. From the Robert Browning poem "Old Pictures in Florence" (Browning 1895, 177).
112. Robinson was assigned to Shimoga in January of 1887 (UTC, "Minutes of the Mysore District Meeting Bangalore Jan. 3rd 1887," in Synod Minutes 1877-1897, C37/B, MMS 21, 353) and had a "native assistant" (Samuel Nathaniel) and five "evangelists" under his oversight (UTC, "Minutes," Dec. 28, 1887, pg. 315).

In the town there was a small church. The Christians were chiefly from other parts. There was a good girls' school in the Brāhman Street, another in the Merchants' Street, a good boys' school, a small school in the dalit hamlet, and the normal school.[113] In the surrounding district there was one girls' school at Davanagere, sixty miles away. In two years, girls' schools were opened at Honnāli, Shikāripura, Soraba, Harihara [Harihar], Tarikere; and also a branch school at Davanagere. I divided the district into three sections, and visited one each month.

At that time I was 120 miles from a railway. No bullocks were to be hired for traveling; I had to buy and keep my own. I took no tea, coffee, or cocoa, no butter nor milk; I used nothing but the barest necessities of life. The bread was very poor. When we were on circuit we had to take it with us; it would become too hard to cut in the dry season, and grow mold nearly an inch thick during the rains.

A New Believer

I believe I baptized the first indigenous merchant caste man in Shimoga.[114] He came to visit me with an evangelist, and we had many conversations and many inquiries. One Saturday he came to my study with his *juttu* (the sacred tuft of hair on the crown of head) shaven off, and said he was ready to give up all and follow Christ.[115] The next day, at the morning service, he was baptized into the Name. He became a teacher in the boys' school. For a time he was one of the most diligent and intelligent students of the scripture, and most faithful in all his duties.

The evangelist with whom he came to me was a Brāhman by birth. When he was in training as an evangelist, some of our Kannadiga men somewhat feared for him. He was led to become a Christian by one of our Kannadiga ministers, who was born a dalit. Many a time we went preaching together, and my study was always open to him and all my helpers.

---

113. On "normal school," see note 6 on page xix.
114. Just what "merchant caste" might mean in today's terms is hard to discern. Presumably it refers to the Vaisya *varna*, which is traditionally associated with business (see note 38 on page 5). L. K. Ananthakrishna Iyer produced an ethnography of Mysore in 1935 that identified eight different Vaisya castes (Singh 2003, xxi, xxxvii).
115. Robinson seems to approve of the act of cutting the sacred tuft of hair, but such changes only confirm that following Christ involves embracing an alternative civilization. Note that the great Tamil Christian poet H. A. Krishna-Pillai never cut his sacred tuft of hair (Devadoss 1946, 38).

Once as we were going to a village, I asked him if a certain sentence he had used was correct. How the fire flashed from his eyes! "Do you say that I, a born Brāhman, make a mistake in speech?"

I asked him to consider if it were not so, meekly suggesting that it was not wise even for a born Brāhman to think he could not make a mistake.

We were good friends. He asked me to dine with him. We sat on the floor in the Brāhman manner. How his birth showed then! I bowed my head in reverence as he taught his wee boy to pray, evidently as usual, and that meal with fingers was to me a benediction.

Once I had to point out, with firm kindliness, some Brāhman tendencies to which by his makeup he was subject, and which caused me much anxiety. He felt, I think, the contrast between them and the commands of our Lord. Before he left my study, he said, "Can we kneel down while you pray, sir?"

I could scarcely pray for thought of the struggle between the old and new, and felt "How hard it is to *be* a Christian!"

At the beginning of my second year the synod was able to appoint an evangelist at Sāgara [Sagar], a western town where no Christian lived, and my born-Brāhman friend was appointed. It was the home of the recent convert. He came, and said he wished to go with the evangelist as colporteur [assistant focused on literature distribution], knowing I was anxious to secure one, so that a man need not be alone. I asked him if he were able to bear his mother's curse. He said he could face everything, and wished most earnestly to go. I was not sure if a man ought to pass through such an ordeal as I knew must face him; but after much thought and prayer I sent them both together.

On the night they reached Sāgara [Sagar], the family of the newly appointed colporteur was performing his *gata shraddhe* (i.e., the burning ceremony for one who has fallen from caste, who is mourned over more than the naturally dead).[116] They had great difficulty in getting any house; the only one they could secure was the home of cobras, in which no one would live. The cobras hung from the bamboos of the roof, hissing at each other. When the evangelist broke the back of one and threw it outside, the people cried out that he was hurting a god. The colporteur had the boys crying out after him, "Have they not burned you tonight?"

---

116. Rarely today does one hear of a death ceremony due to severe violations of caste, although shunning is not unknown.

He bore all bravely, and did his work well. After a while the old life asserted itself; he grew restless, and wished to live in another place. At length he joined the police force, and kept his Christian name.[117] How much of anxiety it meant to enter into and share such soul-struggles!

An Unbaptized Believer

The Brāhman Street was close beside the river, and was, I think, one of the best. There seemed to be a certain spirit in the Brāhmans of Shimoga which won deep regard. The influence of the Brāhman ideal was powerful there. I learned to know many of them, and cherish the memory of their friendship. There was a small Sanskrit school, the teacher of which was a Mādhava Brāhman of the elder type, who most worthily sustained the traditions of his caste. It was a pleasure to hear the pupils recite, but the teaching methods seemed very strange.

There was a *sāstri* (i.e., one who knows the scripture as command) who had learned deep reverence for the Lord Jesus, studied the Gospels carefully, and persuaded many others to do so. Some of his caste called him "*padre*" (i.e., missionary). He did not openly become a Christian, but the influence he exerted among his own people was remarkable.

Interactions with Brāhmans

The commissioner was a Smārta Brāhman, of forceful personality, of insight, and gifted in many ways. A series of English translations of the sacred books was then issued by Brāhmans for the use of Brāhmans alone who could not read Sanskrit. The former apathy in regard to the influence of Christian scripture was gone. There was a determined purpose to learn the best of their own scriptures in order to resist the foreign scripture.

The commissioner kept a *sāstri*, who read the Sanskrit original while he read the English. One day the *sāstri* called at my study, and said he wished to know all about our religious thought. I told him that if he wished to learn

---

117. Apparently this man's name was changed to a "Christian" name when he turned to Christ. No wonder Hindus misunderstood the gospel with practices like this under a colonial government. Nothing more clearly speaks of a change of civilization than a change of name. This practice was already being challenged in Robinson's time, as seen in an 1883 note in *The Harvest Field* in which a Church Missionary Society resolution against the practice is commended (Gleanings 1883, 349-50). Robinson was adopting Hindu dress and diet (Salvation Army people were adopting Indian names and wearing the sacred tuft of hair; see appendix 3), yet he went along with changing the names and appearances of Hindus who turned to Christ.

our religious thought as philosophy or for reasoning, he must learn a few languages, and study their literature. He was quite prepared to do that, as if it were a little thing. Then we talked about our scriptures, and when I said that if he wished to learn our way of redemption it meant the conviction of personal sin, and seeking deliverance from it in faithful obedience to our Lord Jesus, he hissed out, "Your way of thought is too coarse for words."

The old man within me prompted retort, but I tried to learn deeper meekness.

The sessions judge was a Mādhava Brāhman. We had many talks together in his bungalow and in my study. Once, in my study, he said he would like to talk with me as an English gentleman, not as a missionary. I feared the two could hardly be severed, but said I would try. He said, "Do you not really think that at root all religions are one? That beneath many varying forms arising in different countries and after distinctive culture, yet in the root there is unity? May we not say there is so much that is common between yours and ours that there should be no hostility or contradiction?"

I pleaded for consideration of such a large theme, and tried to point out how much it meant. Then he said, "Do you think there is any radical contradiction between your scripture and ours in regard to the real heart-worship of God?"

I asked if he would point out any passage in their scripture which absolutely forbade the worship of God as a spirit by means of material forms as unworthy of God and debasing to men. He replied that I could not think God would reject the worship of a man so trained from childhood, and who could only approach the unseen that way. I suggested that was hardly the point in trying to study the unity or difference of scriptures. Did he know such a prohibition? Then he replied, "Ah! There you talk as a missionary."

I felt he talked as a Brāhman, and how hard it was to reach the man within the man. Yet we talked on, and I tried then, as always, to emphasize the sense of moral failure in the presence of our own ideal, and our need of inward renewal.

There was an elderly Brāhman with whom I often talked. Once he called, bringing with him a student just home from Sringeri. I was trying alone to read some verses of the Rig Veda, and the book lay open on my desk. I pointed to a verse, and asked the student if he would be good enough to read it for me. With a look of horror, he said, "That sacrilege can never be."

He would never let the holy sounds fall from his lips on unpurged ears. The elder looked on in anguish, and lifting up both hands, cried out as if in real pain, "Has not the holy book come into his hands?"

Our talk had to turn away from the Veda that time.

Discussing the Vedas

A *sabha*, or congregation, as we should say, used to meet at that time by invitation at the commissioner's bungalow to discuss the meaning of the sacred books. Teachers of the three Brāhman castes attended regularly to expound, to criticize, and to defend their several interpretations of scripture. The sessions judge and commissioner called upon me one day together. As we talked, the sabha was mentioned, and I was asked if I would attend. "Gladly," I said, "but I do not think your people will suffer my presence when the Veda is read."

They both felt I did not value their influence with their people at its real worth, and said so energetically. I said I was sorry even to seem to undervalue it, but felt only too sure they would never agree to my presence.

The meeting was to be on a Saturday. On the Friday evening the commissioner called to express his great regret that he could not get them to agree to my being present. His own caste, the Smārtas, were willing, but the Mādhavas would not hear of it. After much persuasion they had secured the consent of their chief, the master of the Sanskrit school, and he promised he would try to secure the consent of his caste. The next morning he awoke the household by saying they would put him out of caste if he agreed to that "padre" being there. Teacher and leader as he was, he could not face that threat. I think my friend had not quite grasped all the force of obstruction there. He regretted it, and I certainly did deeply.

The next week, in a Brāhman friend's house, I met the Brāhman who cried out because I possessed the Veda. I asked him how the discussion went on Saturday. All went smoothly, but why didn't I favor them with my presence? Feeling sure he was one who would oppose my invitation, I said, "You are so supremely holy that my shadow would have defiled you."

"Words of scripture," he said reverently, "can only be spoken to those who have the right to hear."

"Was _____ there?" I asked.

"Yes."

"He is a Sudra in caste, though high in government service?"

"Yes."

"What is the penalty appointed for speaking the words of scripture in his ears?"

His face was a study, astute and self-controlled as he was. "It ought not to be," he said several times.

"Was _____ there?"

"Yes."

"He is a heretic, though assistant commissioner?"

"Yes."

"What is the penalty for reciting the Veda in his ears?"

He looked me through and through as I said, "There is no penalty appointed; that sin can never be expiated."

I then reminded him of the Veda he had seen in my study, and said I meant to learn it as far as possible.

Caste Problems

A Brāhman who held the highest honors of Madras University was a good type of the student who uses Western education to defend the ancestral faith. Once he said, "You know such a boys' school. There is a girl there who is very intelligent, and could be trained if opportunity were given. Could you receive her into your own girls' school?"

I asked her caste, and then said, "Where would she live in town?"

"Among her own caste, of necessity."

"What would happen if I suggested she should attend the Brāhman girls' school?"

"Ah!" he exclaimed, and I had to say, "You know, every father who values his caste would take away his girl from any school to which she might be sent."

"Yes, I know."

"Would her mother consent to her being received into one of our boarding schools?"

"That would mean becoming a Christian. No; she would rather die than suffer that."

As we talked together, he pondered the difficulty which arises when you really try to raise one out of the conditions of caste, and he said, "I think it would be a good thing if the lower castes and dalits could become Christians."

On the western hills facing Shimoga mission house, one could discern the far-spreading forests. The evening star was so clear it could be seen shining through the trees and dipping behind the hill. In those parts of my circuit we had no evangelist, and there was no possibility of regular visits for teaching. At every point, work was urgent and clamorous; but though we all did our utmost, it was hopelessly beyond our power to compass it. I used to look across the west and pray that God would work in the hearts of men whom we were quite unable to reach. Everything one did seemed but to show how vastly more was undone.

Investing in Students

But my whole self was given in hardest work to the normal students. There were twenty of them. I felt it would be of little avail to teach them the theories of teaching. They would teach in imitation of the method in which they were taught. So I taught them three hours a day, five days a week, and crowded my circuit journeys into the nights and days remaining, so as to cause the least possible disturbance to their studies. Usually it was considered absolutely necessary to do receptive work during the hottest part of the day. I taught them in Kannada, never a word of English, with nothing but tiles to shield us from the sun.

Textbooks were a great difficulty. We had no satisfactory commentary on the New Testament in Kannada. The second catechism was translated, but had [already] then been learned.[118] If there was to be efficient teaching, the preparation of textbooks was a prime necessity. I wrote an explanatory translation of St. John's Gospel, with notes, and an adaptation of W. B. Pope's

---

118. The second Methodist catechism was a summary of Christian doctrine and Bible history; the first catechism was for children (Wesleyan Methodist Church 1800s).

Higher Catechism for the seniors. For the juniors I began a historical scripture catechism; I translated into Kannada the Bombay government first and second Sanskrit-English books, with fuller exercises, and part of Paul Bert's *First Year of Scientific Knowledge.* My students had to copy my manuscript; I could not print as the work went on.

The response of those students was, and is, one of the greatest blessings of my life. I felt if they were to be true teachers, the Lord Jesus Himself must become the center-force of personality, so I asked if they were quite willing to learn one verse of His words every day, and repeat the seven for each week on the Sunday. They agreed gladly, and every Sunday evening I was at home we all met together after service, and each repeated his seven verses.

I tried to work so that preaching or visiting schools should not be lessened. Many a time I had to force myself when the need for rest was more clamorous than usual. More than once I taught half-lying down, because pain would not suffer me to stand.[119]

---

119. This looks like a clear reference to a chronic illness, but no explanation is ever given.

Chapter 6

Final Years of Brokenness

*In the depression of those days
the outlook was too dark even for despair.*

—Benjamin Robinson

"Whoso suffers most hath most to give."[120]

DEBILITATING ILLNESS

At the end of July, 1889, we went from Shimoga to visit evangelists and schools, and preach on the eastern side of the circuit. When forty miles away from home, the west wind, for which I had so often wished as the breath of life, caused me to shiver.[121] We reached Harihara [Harihar] after dark. During the night, violent internal pain seized me, and I was helpless. There was a hospital assistant ten miles away, who was sent for. He said I had severe congestion of the liver, and advised going into Bangalore for treatment.

---

120. This is the closing line of a poem by Harriet Eleanor Hamilton-King (1840-1920). See http://www.bartleby.com/293/232.html.
121. Monsoon season in July can certainly bring chilly weather. This third breakdown in health proved extremely costly for Robinson. In their annual letter to the missionaries in south India of October 21, 1889, the WMMS board in London stated,

> The Committee must strongly impress upon the brethren the obligation to take all reasonable care of their health. Young missionaries are apt to presume upon their fresh strength & to disregard the experience of older residents with regard to diet, dress & exposure in the climate. The Committee cannot but think that Mr. Robinson, though a brother of experience, put too severe a strain upon his constitution in making his recent tour under such conditions of hardship & exposure. (UTC, "Minutes of Mysore District Meeting Bangalore Jan 2nd 1890," in Synod Minutes 1877-1897, C37/B, MMS 21, copy of an unsigned letter from Wesleyan Mission House London to Rev. Josiah Hudson, chairman and general superintendent of the Mysore district, October 21, 1889, 442)

> Robinson's record of his service does not indicate any extreme risks taken after the first round of barefoot itineration from Gubbi in 1885. But notice the comment just below about "fasting and rigorous abstinence such as I tried."

A fortnight afterwards the Southern Mahratta Railway was opened to Bangalore, and I was saved the fatigue and pain of 120 miles' journey by bullock cart. We hoped that with medical treatment and the drier climate it would soon be possible to resume work, but we never returned to Shimoga. The doctor said I was suffering from neurasthenia and hepatitis, and ordered me home at once. I pleaded for my work, broken in the midst, and begged that something might be tried where I was. But they spoke, very decisively. "No; home or …"[122]

When I was carried aboard ship, my faithful servant, who had been with me on most of my journeys during the seven years, said with tears that he hoped I should soon be well and return.[123] He would look out for me, and be glad to live with us again.

They helped me on deck, to lie down there, day by day. The charm and freshness of the sea lessened my pain, and I was able to walk the deck's length when we reached the Mediterranean, and began to hope; but when we had landed, and the first excitement was over, I had constant pain, and fainted several times every day; also always if I attempted any short walk.

---

122. Hudson wrote to London on August 24, saying,

> I very much regret to have to inform you that Mr. Robinson is ordered home by the doctors. A little more than three weeks ago Mr. Robinson accompanied by Mrs. R. left Shimoga to visit several outstations. On arriving at Harihar he became very ill. He sent to Davanagere, 9 miles distance, for the native hospital assistant, who found that his liver was much congested and enlarged. As soon as I received the news I telegraphed to him to come to Bangalore. (SOAS Library, WMMS India Correspondence Mysore 1879-1895 box #34, microfiche number 1495, Aug. 24, 1889, letter from J. Hudson to J. Walton)

> Reports in *The Harvest Field* emphasized in September that Robinson hoped to stay and then in October that he desired to return:

> We regret to hear that the Rev. R. [sic] Robinson, of Shimoga, whose "Experiment in Mission Work" has lately interested so many of our readers, is seriously ill and has been ordered by the doctors to return to England. His absence at present will create a grave difficulty, as he is at the head of the work in one of the most extensive districts in the Mysore country. We trust that his medical advisers may yet see some sudden improvement which will justify them in permitting him to labour, as he wishes, for some time longer before taking a change. (Notes 1889, 119)

> The Rev. B. Robinson sailed on the 19th ultimo for England. Up to that date he had become no better, but rather worse, and the doctors were quite decided that no other course was open to them but to send him home. Mr. Robinson is fully bent on returning to his work (D.V.) as soon as his health is sufficiently restored. He is a most efficient vernacular preacher, and we are greatly weakened by his absence. (Mysore 1889, 141)

123. September 19, 1889, was the date Robinson was finally well enough to board a ship and sail (SOAS Library, WMMS India Correspondence Mysore 1879-1895 box #34, microfiche number 1495, letter from J. Hudson to J. Walton, Aug. 24, 1889). A report from 1890 pointed out that "In August, Mr. Robinson broke down so completely that it was only after weeks of intense suffering and with the greatest care that he could proceed to England" (SOAS Library, WMMS Reports Vol. XXIV, 1888-1890, "Report for the year ending Dec. 31st, 1889" [1890 report, page 67, no authorship attributed]).

For three years I lay in utter powerlessness, with pain that knew no ease. There was no sleep; or if, when I could bear no more, sleep came in the early morning, within half an hour I would awake, teaching or preaching in Kannada, or shuddering with frightful dreams. In the depression of those days the outlook was too dark even for despair.

After three years I began to meet a class for religious fellowship in our home, and visited the sick and poor. In the fifth year I began, trembling, to preach in English once a week. There was perpetual pain of mind as I preached; I had grown to feel far more at home with Kannada than English, and the comparison always included a reference to the work left undone in Karnataka.

The physician would not suffer me to attempt the night exposure of traveling after preaching, so there came seven years of country charges in Scotland as one's only hope of gaining back something of health. Sometimes I hoped strength enough to return to Karnataka would be given, but the physician said that must not enter my dreams. Then I hoped for sufficient vigor to study and work up to the limit of my desire at home, but pain has seldom been far away, and nerve weakness has always been ready to warn.

Reflections on the India Years

Through the years I look back upon that seven years' experiment, only fairly begun when it was broken, and left unfinished. It seemed as if I were just gaining insight and sympathy enough to do effective work in bringing the mind of Christ to the minds of men, and then all that I gained was thrust aside, as if seemingly useless. Do the conclusions I reached in Karnataka stand the test of all the thought which years of pain have brought?

I still feel that change of dress in Karnataka hinders the real work of reaching the hearts of the Kannadiga people. Caste is birth, it cannot be assumed. If native food alone be eaten, it will lower vitality and render work at European standards impossible; yet I would not eat beef or pork. It is possible that fasting and rigorous abstinence such as I tried may so weaken a man working to the limit of his strength that there may be grave peril to his life; yet I would live as simply and frugally as possible for health and efficient service. Religion is not meat and drink, not anything outward; but the mind of Christ. If the religion of Jesus became a caste![124]

---

124. This is a striking exclamation that reveals a deep fear of syncretism. In fact, by "refusing compromise with caste" the standard pattern of nineteenth-century mission work pulled people from their castes, which in effect made them into a new social group, a new caste. Only by followers of Christ remaining within their castes could the followers of Jesus have avoided becoming a caste group.

The moral and spiritual quality of personality will count here. The ideal man of the Vedic faiths is the *sadhu*—the meek, gentle, gracious man who has conquered desire so that he may be helpful. "The gentle are kind even to despicable animals. Does the moon withhold light from dalit huts?" "He who is gentle to the helpful, what virtue has his gentleness? He who is gentle to the hurtful, he alone is gentle, so the wise affirm."[125] In the ferment of faiths and civilizations, in the midst of conflicting ideals, the meek, gentle, self-sacrificing goodness of Jesus appeals to the heart of Brāhman and dalit, in spite of the differences and failure of those who bear His name.

The deepest question of all to me is—How far was I Christlike in spirit in the toil and testing of those seven years? May merits be weighed, offenses pardoned? Out of all the years of pain there has grown the certainty that he who would help uplift men must have as much of the mind of Christ as God can give to those who count all loss to gain Christlikeness.

Was it worthwhile to live and labor thus, and to suffer through doing so? If measured by gain or health, it was all loss. But if we measure "by the wine poured forth, not by the wine drank,"[126] if the cross of our Savior be the symbol of the Spirit that is evolving goodness in the race of man, it was the loss that alone is gain.

There was an ancient sage who retired to the forest, and lived in study there till the divine and eternal so grew upon his thought that he felt all words could speak no more. He lived in solitary silence, pondering the ineffable. Another sage, anxious to gain the true knowledge of the supreme reality that leads man to his goal, came to him in the forest to be his disciple, and earnestly begged to be taught the supreme reality. The sage continued silent. At length the disciple said, "I begged to be taught, and you never uttered a word."

Then the teacher said, "I am teaching all the time in the only true way, but you do not understand."

The disciple felt, too, that the deepest and highest devotion is dumb in the presence of the divine, which is above all speech and thought.[127] Yet the divine law says, "Truth is better than silence."[128]

---

125. I have been unable to locate these quotations.
126. From the same poem as the quote that opens this chapter.
127. This is a common story with many variations. Swami Krishnananda tells it in his exposition of the Mandukya Upanishad (1977, 113).
128. The statement that truth is better than silence is neither a biblical nor a Sanskrit axiom, but it is consistent with the teaching of both traditions. The statement seems to contrast with the preceding story, and seems to me to be Robinson's apologia for writing his account. He could have kept silence, but felt a higher calling to speak truth.

Lead us from the unreal to the real,

Lead us from darkness to light,

Lead us from death to deathless life.[129]

---

129. Bṛhadāranyaka Upanishad 1.3.28.

Afterword

Benjamin's Robinson's moving account of his failed missionary service stirs many thoughts about the meaning of Christ and "Christian mission" today. I hope my afterthoughts might help stir others' thoughts and discussions. Currently, the development of a global church is being celebrated, yet with recognition that vast segments of the global human community remain far from Christ. Eurocentric Christianity must give way to contextual expressions of discipleship to Jesus if all peoples are indeed to hear of and follow Christ. Robinson made a heroic attempt in this direction; hope for current success in India lies not with Europeans who follow Robinson's example, but with Hindus who follow Christ within their own cultural and caste contexts.

My personal encounter with India began with deep involvement with Indian Christianity, initially just in literature distribution among Hindus and Muslims. I found a niche among Indian Christians as a teacher of the Bible, which I attempted to do without Western illustrations or thought patterns. In hindsight, I had no idea how to transcend a Western approach to the Bible; I am still only a beginner in that. After nearly a decade in India I was introduced to the remarkable stream of those (like Benjamin Robinson and Henry Haigh) who sought to rethink the meaning and practice of Christ in light of Hindu contexts. That introduction was from Acharya Daya Prakash Titus, and my brief encounter with him changed the entire direction of my life.

Like Benjamin Robinson, I changed my diet and dress in order to more closely identify with classical Hindu traditions. Like Robinson, I began a deep study of Indian thought. But my early years in this endeavor, exactly a century after Robinson, were in a very different India than his India (and India at the time of this writing is very different again from the India of the late 1980s). I was and am linguistically challenged, and although I now regret not working seriously at acquiring an Indian language or two, academic work related to Hindu traditions is overwhelmingly in English. I was never tempted to attempt the role of guru or evangelist, going among people like Robinson did, particularly due to some friends who were genuine Hindus who could do that with vastly more insight and integrity than I could ever have mustered.

So I could not write an account anywhere near like Robinson's. My encounters with Hindu traditions are quite secondhand—through books or through Hindu friends who followed Jesus, the latter either telling about their own experiences in a Hindu family or recounting stories of other Hindus they encountered. My academic studies never focused on a single Hindu *sampradāya* (sect/denomination), and anything resembling expertise only developed in the field of the historical engagement between Protestant Christian and Hindu traditions. Obviously, it was during investigations in this field that I came across Benjamin Robinson and his book.

Robinson's dismay at the vast diversity of Hindu traditions points to an essential insight; there is no one expression of discipleship to Jesus that will appeal to all Hindus. The dynamics of Hindu traditions reveal multiple developments under the inspiration of diverse individuals, and a similar dynamic must be expected when Jesus is embraced as guru. The multifaceted character of the genius of Christ has never been adequately embraced in Western Christian traditions, which have instead sought a single essence or focus, thus contributing to the fragmentation of Christianity into thousands of denominations and sects. Hopefully the often-esteemed tolerance of Hindu traditions will lead to a more respectful interaction of different expressions of discipleship to Jesus in Hindu contexts.

Where it seems Robinson missed out, as mentioned in my introduction, was in recognition of the significance of, and then radical initiatives related to, the Hindus he met who expressed sincere regard, even devotion, for Jesus, yet who confessed an inability to embrace Christianity. How tragic that even a seeker like Benjamin Robinson was blinded by the inadequate paradigm that one must "change religion" to be a follower of Jesus. Might Robinson have learned a better way, might he have seen how historically conditioned (rather than biblically based) this perspective was, if he had had longer to wrestle with these issues?

Hindsight is clear that Robinson went further than he needed to when he started walking barefoot through rural Karnataka in the intensity of summer. I hold this conclusion despite Robinson's claim, "Yet I do not know how I could have reached the point from which I could gain the necessary insight if I had not made that experiment" (pg. 29). Granting his conclusion on this point, severe criticism falls on his supervisors who kept this man busy in schools instead of freeing him to conduct his experiment in a more sensible season of the year. There is a larger problem here also, in the general missionary embrace of itineration as an approach to people; opportunities for deep engagement with individuals were passed by in favor of superficial encounters with thousands.[130]

Maybe Benjamin Robinson, growing from year to year in India, still would not have far transcended his times; maybe he would not have heard of Kandiswamy Chetti in Madras, who followed Jesus without converting to Christianity; maybe he would have been enticed by Farquhar's fulfillment thesis and been distracted from the more holistic contextualization that is evidenced in embryo in his record republished here. Robinson's shortened career is one of many stories that stimulate the student of history and instill regrets that the further story never developed.

History compels imaginings about the future. In roughly another century from now, in 2112, not only will Robinson's account be an old history with many quirks and dated interpretations, but the introduction and notes and afterword of this retelling will also be seen to contain comic errors in perspective and perhaps tragic lack of insight. As the psalmist said, a thousand ages in God's sight are like a watch in the night, while an individual human life passes by like a plant withering in a day (Psalm 90:4–6). God gives us few (if any) glimpses into what is truly valid and lasting in our thoughts and actions, a deeply humbling thought that, if embraced, should reduce the number of books and podcasts!

Yet somehow the record that Benjamin Robinson wrote of his struggles with Hindu contexts stands the test of time. There is an honesty that is all too rare in the annals of expansionist Christianity. There is vision and compassion and a refusal to accept the status quo. But there is deep humility, a deep

---

130. Itineration in the hot season continued to be a mission practice, as seen in this statement from the annual report for 1888:
> Tours for evangelistic purposes are arranged whenever practicable. Last hot weather, for instance, one missionary, accompanied by two evangelists, and two Christian teachers, *walked* through a somewhat neglected part of the district, away from the high roads, stopping at every village or hamlet to which they came. They took pains to collect all the people available, and set themselves leisurely to the most patient explanation and the most energetic appeal. They planned no distance to be covered each day. They lingered wherever opportunity invited, took their meals as they could by the side of a stream or tank, and at night slept under trees, or in the verandah of a temple, or in a common bullock cart, just as convenience suggested. (SOAS Library, WMMS Reports Vol. XXIV, 1888-1890, report for 1888, 68; italics original)

There is no reason to think this was anyone other than Benjamin Robinson; at the very least it was someone impacted by Robinson's experiences.

commitment to learn, an exemplary sense of inadequacy for a high calling. One can be excused for hoping that similar traits are obvious when our own record is studied after the passing of another century. I feel I am a better person and a better disciple of Jesus for having encountered Benjamin Robinson in the pages of this book; I hope this change is evident to others, and I pray a similar experience and encounter for many others—thus this reprint of Robinson's record of his experiences.

Appendix 1
Reviews of the First Edition of This Book

Two reviews of Robinson's book will be reproduced here. The first and longest was published in the *International Review of Missions* and helped set the narrative that Robinson's approach to mission should never be attempted again. The second is much more sympathetic, coming from Robinson's south Indian Methodist mission colleagues who produced *The Harvest Field*.

Review 1: Caste and the Missionary, a review of *In the Brāhmans' Holy Land* by J. O. F. Murray of Selwyn College, Cambridge, *International Review of Missions* vol. 2 no. 3, 1913, pages 609–10

The importance of this book is not to be measured by its size. It is the record of a costly experiment made humbly and with whole-hearted self-surrender, and so, even when it seemed to fail, establishing conclusions of far-reaching significance.

The problem set before all missionaries is to discover means whereby they can bridge the gulf which divides them as strangers and foreigners from those whom they are longing to bring to the feet of their Master. This book throws fresh light on the stupendous difficulty of that problem in India. For here is the story of a man filled with the true missionary spirit: devoting himself without stint to the task set before him: studying the language of his people till he thought and dreamt in it: saturating himself in their sacred literature: watchful to cast out of his own life anything that might offend their susceptibilities: making himself as far as possible, even to the ruin of his own health, one with them in food and dress: feeling their sins as a burden on his own conscience before God. And the net result of all his striving seems at first sight to be merely negative: "Change of dress in Mysore hinders the real work of reaching the hearts of the Kanarese people." Yet even if this were all, we may make bold to say that the experiment was worthwhile. It has been made once for all. Loving hearts and sensitive consciences need never tread that path again.[131]

But this is not all. The effort to draw nearer heart to heart with his Indian brothers brought with it clearer insight into the meaning and power of that institution which for three thousand years has been the dominant factor in the life and thought of Hindustan. "Caste is birth and cannot be assumed." To those who are under its sway it is of direct divine appointment. The thought of it is closely knit into one with all their faith in God. And yet caste so consecrates the bond which unites all who share a common blood, and feed on common food, as to exclude the possibility of any wider brotherhood, and makes them feel that it is a profanation to share the knowledge even of their sacred scriptures with an outsider.[132] The facts no doubt are familiar, but we cannot but be grateful for any experience that enables us to realize them once more in their awful intensity. Hinduism is a fortress in our Promised Land too strongly entrenched and too vigilantly guarded to be taken by direct assault. And clear insight into the nature of the task of reducing it is necessary if weak hearts are not to faint "with weary looking for the day." For siege operations are necessarily slow, and may easily seem to be making no progress up to the very moment of the final triumph. A fortress falls altogether if it falls at all.[133]

Review 2: A review of *In the Brāhmans' Holy Land* in *The Harvest Field*, March 1913, page 113

This book, which can be read through in a couple of hours, is one of the few books that are self revealing. It is the story of one who tried to get into closest touch with the people, by adopting their dress, their food, and manner of life. Sincerity, loyalty to Jesus Christ, and devotion to duty are impressed upon this human document. It is, however, the story of a failure. In spite of change of habits, caste was an impassable barrier and prevented the sharing of the inner domestic and social life of the people. Young missionaries, eager to deny

---

131. This seems a shocking conclusion. Was the expectation that the whole world would follow Western Christianity?
132. Both the premises and the conclusions of these statements are based on a simplistic understanding of caste.
133. This is reminiscent of Alexander Duff's famous analogy of Hinduism as a rock that must be dynamited, and fails for the same reason. As John McKenzie pointed out in critiquing Duff, "Hinduism was proved to be not a mass of rock that might be mined and blown up, but a living plant with many roots, that was capable of eluding the art of the sapper and miner" (1929, 91).

themselves and anxious to bring the message of Christ home to the people, may well ponder the story here presented. The way of approach to the Hindu is not by changing habits of living, but by so studying his ways of thought and especially the higher aspects of Hinduism that the missionary may get into mental touch with those to whom he has to present Christ. Though no one is so expert in matters of external form as the Hindu, yet he knows as well as any that external change does not necessarily mean an inward change as well. Mr. Robinson has done well in baring his soul for the benefit of those who come after.

Appendix 2
Benjamin Robinson's Engagement and Marriage

In the midst of his physical anguish after his summer evangelistic tour, Robinson noted, as recorded in the first paragraph of chapter 3, that he "had to face alone life's task and meaning." He did not mention there that he had a fiancée in England who was unable to join him due to health problems. Some details about that relationship, and about his marriage to a different woman nine months before leaving India, can be traced in correspondence in the Methodist Mission archives at the School of Oriental and African Studies in London. (Note that the letters below are not strictly in chronological order; the excerpt that describes the illness of Robinson's fiancée is second below, but it is from a later letter than some others that follow.)

The first mention of Robinson's fiancée, who is only called Miss Hinch in the archival records, appears in a letter written on July 7, 1886, from Robinson's field advisor, Josiah Hudson, in Bangalore, to London Wesleyan Methodist Missionary Society foreign secretary Ebenezer E. Jenkins. This letter also shows the esteem in which Robinson was held by his colleagues, and also their concern at his zeal perhaps leading to unwise actions.

> I have had a good deal of talk and correspondence with Robinson about his engagement. I have urged him to get it formally broken off, and not improbably he will succeed in doing so, but he does not feel himself at all free to marry. The lady says he must marry if he thinks it is God's will that he should do so, but she intimates at the same time that she is unable to feel it is God's will she should give him up. Under these circumstances Robinson feels he can do nothing….

> Unfortunately as soon as he gives up the thought of marriage he instinctively flies to asceticism. I believe that if the lady had the faintest idea of the fight he has continually to make she would not hesitate an hour. He wrote about become a supernumerary—living upon the alms of the people—working in the villages outside of all circuit organizations. I wrote to him very plainly, telling him that he proposed laying upon himself a burden he was utterly unable to bear, and that he would either ruin his health, or unhinge his mind, or drive himself to despair. I suggested that it would be better to seek relief in the very opposite way, and that he might look out for some young man like-minded with himself with whom he might share his salary and work. You will see from the enclosed letter that he was delighted at this suggestion, and that he is quite willing to share with a brother everything he has got....
>
> The life would be rough enough, but not I think unhealthy, except there were a special tendency to fever. I cannot imagine any better preparation for mission life than three or four years with a man who has gained such an extraordinary knowledge of the language and modes of thought of the people. A superficial, lifeless, luxurious sort of man, would be miserable enough in Robinson's company, but a thoroughly intelligent and earnest missionary would have unexampled opportunities for learning his business. I have no doubt there are men both suitable and willing to come if they could only be found out. Robinson would be much pained if there were any public appeal for a co-worker—he could not bear that at all—but he does not object to a private search. (SOAS Library, WMMS India Correspondence Mysore 1879–1895, box #34, microfiche 1489, letter number 7, July 24, 1886; letter from J. Hudson to E. E. Jenkins; the referenced "enclosed letter" is not in the archival collection)

The root problem becomes clear in a letter written over a year later on October 23, 1887, again from Hudson in Bangalore to Jenkins in London. This was a response to rumors that Robinson was making excuses to get out of his engagement with Miss Hinch.

> I think Miss Hinch's friends do not know what a very serious view Robinson took of her health. I understand that she had some heart affection and there is no doubt that before leaving England Robinson was persuaded her health was seriously if not dangerously affected. This view of the case was confirmed by letters infrequently received from Miss Hinch, as well as by other news from Wellingborough. If I remember rightly one winter Miss Hinch was confined to her house for three or four months. Robinson judged from some expression used by Miss Hinch herself that her life had been in danger, and he certainly feared she would not live long. Under these

circumstances he fully believed that it would be wrong to marry, and that if no other course came open to him he must remain permanently a bachelor. (SOAS Library, WMMS India Correspondence Mysore 1879–1895, box #34, microfiche 1489, letter number 39, Oct. 23, 1887, letter from J. Hudson to E. E. Jenkins)

The following letter, again from Hudson to Jenkins but earlier (July 16, 1887) than the one just quoted, refers to complaints from friends of Miss Hinch and in response provides a strong character witness for Robinson:

> Mr. Sawday speaks very plainly about the opinion of the people at Wellingborough. They do not believe that Robinson assigns the real reason when he speaks of ill-health as the obstacle to marriage. They think that his objection arises from Miss Hinch's lack of education and refinement. Mr. Sawday thinks that some of her friends would be disposed to lay the case before the [Methodist] Conference if the engagement were broken off.… I believe few men are more perfectly sincere and conscientious than Robinson. He would be the last man to do anything unkind or dishonourable. At the same time his judgement about Miss H's health may have been unconsciously biased by his sense of her unfitness in other respects. (SOAS Library, WMMS India Correspondence Mysore 1879–1895, box #34, microfiche number 1492, letter number 34; J. Hudson letter of July 16, 1887, to E. E. Jenkins)

Robinson himself had written to Jenkins in London on January 10, 1887, clearly with hope that Miss Hinch would be able to join him in India.

> Miss Hinch wrote again last week and while not deciding to come, she seems more inclined to consider it than she did. The medical exam seems to hinder her a little.… I am anxious that if it be possible she should come out before the hot weather & should be glad if you will do anything you can to urge her to come at once if that be possible. You will I know do all you can to relieve me of the uncertainty & pain of my present position. (SOAS Library, WMMS India Correspondence Mysore 1879–1895 box #34, microfiche number 1491, letter number 20).

In light of the possible travel of Miss Hinch to join Robinson in India, Hudson wrote to Jenkins on March 29, 1887, giving his hesitant approval:

> It is now perfectly plain that Robinson cannot marry anyone else. He would feel that he was acting unkindly to Miss Hinch and could neither be happy himself, nor make anyone else happy. This is quite clear from his last letter on the subject. And yet Robinson is likely to break down if he continues as he is. If the doctor gives you any hope of Miss Hinch being able to bear the

climate it seems to me to be the best to let her come. But I acknowledge that if this is the best alternative it is at the same time a bad one. (SOAS Library, WMMS India Correspondence Mysore 1879–1895, box #34, microfiche number 1491, letter number 25)

In an almost indecipherable letter (Robinson's letters seem to have been written on cheaper paper than Hudson's), Robinson wrote to Jenkins on July 22, 1887, that his situation in Shimoga had convinced him that he needed to marry so that his wife could take advantage of many opportunities among Hindu women there (SOAS Library, WMMS India Correspondence Mysore 1879–1895, box #34, microfiche number 1492, letter number 35, July 22, 1887, letter from Robinson to Jenkins).

Josiah Hudson's letter to Jenkins of October 23, 1887, has been quoted above as it gives the best picture of the health problems of Miss Hinch. In that letter, Hudson goes on to again support Miss Hinch's coming to India and marrying Robinson, and describes Robinson's dilemma in his relationship with her. (Hudson's handwriting is difficult and some words are not decipherable on the microfiche.)

> I think now that he [Robinson] made a great mistake in not inquiring further into the matter of health before leaving England. Probably Miss Hinch's heart affection was only functional, arising from general health[?] but functional derangement is often very distressing and Robinson might well believe that there is organic disease.
>
> The six months' silence you refer to must have been between the arrival of the letter from Mr. Ferize and that from Mr. Sawday. He [Robinson] did not know what to do. He has been writing to me frequently on the subject and he seemed about in despair as to the course he should take. He feared to make matters worse by writing as he could not easily overcome his fears about health. It was a pity he did not write, but his position was difficult enough. I should add he was waiting for the result of the [medical] examination.
>
> I scarcely think Robinson is to blame for the present delay. He was greatly [?] to hear from Miss Hinch that she [?] He thought he had made his wishes quite plain. I have no doubt that he has written still more plainly since.
>
> I wrote last week that he would like her to come out as soon as possible, before the cold weather sets in.
>
> We shall give Miss Hinch a hearty welcome. She need not doubt Robinson's affection for her. Even when he believed he could not marry her he often felt that his affection for her would make it wrong for him to marry anybody else.

I hope you will be able to satisfy his friends—rather her friends—that Robinson is not changed from what he was in former days. (SOAS Library, WMMS India Correspondence Mysore 1879–1895, box #34, microfiche 1489, letter number 39, Oct. 23, 1887; letter from J. Hudson to E. E. Jenkins)

But in late 1887 or early 1888 it is clear that Miss Hinch made a final decision that she would not travel to India, and she freed Robinson from any commitments he had made to her. This is clear in a letter of February 16, 1888, from Jenkins to Robinson.

> Feb 16/88
> Dear Brother Robinson,
> Upon receiving your last letter I wrote to Miss Hinch assuring her that she was at liberty to dispense with the medical opinion; and that I would make every arrangement for her comfortable embarkation and voyage. I enclosed the letter or rather addressed it to the care of Mr. Bate.
>
> He replied in her name giving me hope that she would consent to leave England at once. But another letter from Mr. Bate disappointed my expectation. I enclose both these letters because it is important you should have them: also the doctor opinions. I am sorry dear brother for your sake that a long cherished wish has failed. But I am thankful for Miss Hinch's sake and yours that, at any rate, the period of doubt and suspense has expired. You are now free from either.
>
> I am writing a word to comfort Miss Hinch: for to her the breaking up finally of an engagement which has filled with hope many years of her life is, as you know, a very heavy trial. (SOAS Library, India MMS/Home/Correspondence/FBN 32, microfiche number 1637, letter number 35, Feb. 16, 1888; the referenced enclosed letters are not part of the archival collection)

Robinson's response to Jenkins on March 10, 1888, provides further light on the ending of their relationship. Since the top and bottom portions of this three-page letter are not decipherable, only part of the letter can be quoted.

> Thank you very much for writing to Miss Hinch. It must be an unspeakably severe trial to her and I can only pray that she may have God's unspeakable blessing. In her letter which came this morning she says the doctor told her more than he could tell you and adds "I do with tears in my eyes and a heart full of love to you say, 'please try & marry some one else who will be a help to you in every way & I will pray for you and love you all my days.'" Her Christlike unselfishness has always been an immeasurable help to me but it has never been so conspicuous as in this severe trial and my appreciation for

> her is greater if possible. I have told her that it would be more to my mind to remain as I am than think of anyone else.... (SOAS Library, WMMS India Correspondence Mysore 1879–1895 box #34, microfiche number 1493, letter number 46)

Robinson goes on to affirm a duty to Miss Hinch, but also asks for Jenkins' advice about marriage. That Robinson's supervisors wanted him to marry is clear from the letters above, and the decisive break had now been made from Miss Hinch. It is in a letter five months later, from Robinson to Jenkins on August 23, 1888, that we learn that Robinson would marry Miss I. Britten, daughter of the late Henry B. Britten (1825–87) (SOAS Library, WMMS India Correspondence Mysore 1879–1895, box #34, microfiche number 1495, letter number 61).

I was able to locate neither a date for Robinson's marriage nor the first name of his wife. The SOAS archival staff kindly provided for me the full name and dates of Miss Britten's father, but they only learned about her marriage to Robinson from me. The letter quoted below expresses the hope that Miss Britten will arrive in India before Christmas in 1888. The January 1889 issue of *The Harvest Field* includes this statement: "In the Mysore Mission two of the brethren have been married during the month—the Rev. B. Robinson to Miss Britton of Sittingbourne, and the Rev. W. W. Holdsworth, m. a. to Miss Williams of Croydon" (Personalia 1889, 241). Thus Robinson married either at the very end of 1888 or in January 1889.

This final letter brings the saga of Robinson's broken engagement and marriage to a fitting end. It was written on October 9, 1888, by Josiah Hudson to John Walton, who earlier in 1888 had replaced the retired E. E. Jenkins as foreign secretary of the WMMS.

> Mr. Robinson asks me to write to you about Miss Britten, the lady to whom he has just been engaged. He is anxious she should come out with one of the missionary partners before Christmas. I have only heard of the engagement since last mail went out, so that I could not write earlier, but Mr. Robinson tells me he sent Miss Britten a letter to forward to you in case she determined to come out. Mr. Robinson has travelled ten years and of course might have married long before this, but the lady to whom he was formerly engaged had to break off the connection on account of serious ill health. Mr. Jenkins knows all the circumstances and will be glad to hear that Robinson's troubles seem now at an end. (SOAS Library, WMMS India Correspondence Mysore 1879–1895, box #34, microfiche number 1495, letter number 64)

Appendix 3
The Missionary Lifestyle Debate in *The Harvest Field*

In light of the importance of lifestyle questions in Benjamin Robinson's record of his service, this appendix presents a survey of opinions published in *The Harvest Field* from the early 1880s into the early 1890s. The Salvation Army became the center of the debate, as will be obvious below. This is important background information for a proper analysis of Robinson and his legacy.

The Harvest Field was a journal that failed in its first attempt in the 1860s, but after a relaunch in July of 1880 it developed into one of the premier journals of the missionary community in India. When the National Christian Council of India was organized in 1914, the Wesleyan Methodists of south India generously offered *The Harvest Field* to become the official journal of the new council. This was formally accepted only in 1923, and the name was changed to *The National Christian Council Review*.

In September of 1881, in a section entitled "Notes of Other Churches and Societies" (i.e., other than the Methodists), an interesting incident was noted.

> One of the members of the Oxford Mission in Calcutta has adopted the native dress. The *Sunday Mirror* admires his moral courage, (*sic*), other critics appear to regard the adoption as verging on the ridiculous. Perhaps it is only fair, that as in Calcutta the Babu approximates to the Englishman in his dress, so the educated Englishman should approximate to the Hindu, and repay the compliment of his Eastern brother. (*The Harvest Field*, second series, vol. 2 no. 3, Sept. 1881: 93)

The *sic* in this statement is in the original, and contributes to the mocking tone of the whole. "Adopting the native dress" was not a subject to take seriously, rather a distraction good for a few laughs. But a year later that changed with the arrival of the Salvation Army and their embrace of local dress and diet, which was part of a larger criticism of the traditional mission enterprise.

The Salvation Army never hid their theological affiliation with Wesleyan Methodists, founder William Booth famously stating that "to me there was one God, and John Wesley was his prophet." *The Harvest Field* of July and August of 1882 published a two-part introduction to the Salvation Army which was highly commendatory, and also in that August issue shared the news that Frederick Tucker (who changed his name to Booth-Tucker when he married William Booth's second daughter in April of 1888) would be bringing the Army's work to India.

"We are sure that all earnest Christians will welcome their coming," said the article, which also gave the information that the Army uniform in India would be yellow in color (*The Harvest Field,* second series, vol. 3 no. 2, Aug. 1882: 63). The commendatory tone continued in a few later notices in September and October of 1882.

In June of 1884 *The Harvest Field* noted without comment that the Salvation Army had taken radical steps of adaptation in India.

> The Salvation Army holds that adaptation is, under God, a primary element of success, and Major Tucker has so far acted on that principle as to discard shoes and walk the roads barefooted. The natives think that he has now begun to approach the ideal of an Indian faqir and honour him for it. (p. 378)

After two other brief notices, at the bottom of that same page begins the first criticism of the Salvation Army in India. In Gujarat some missionaries had gone public with criticism of sheep-stealing and related problems, and *The Harvest Field* gave extensive quotations of the criticisms. It concluded that news piece by saying,

> All this is sad, if true; and we should like to believe that Major Tucker's enthusiasm has led him to act, not with guile, but without discrimination.... All the same Major Tucker is seriously blameworthy; yet instead of rebutting the charges or acknowledging his mistake, he prefers to pose as the martyr, persecuted by the unworthy jealousy of brethren less holy than himself! (*The Harvest Field*, second series, vol. 4 no. 12, June 1884: 380)

The broader controversies about the Salvation Army were often discussed in the following years in *The Harvest Field*, but that is beyond the purview of this appendix. It did not take long, however, for *The Harvest Field* to pick up on the issue of the missionary lifestyle in light of the challenge from the Army.

Just a month after noting Tucker's barefooted approach, in July of 1884, under "Notes and Extracts," there are critical comments about the book *Five Years of Faith Work in India*, by C. B. Ward of the Telugu Faith Mission. The book commends assimilation to the local lifestyle, and the review comments that Tucker is operating on the same principle as Ward, but is carrying it to extremes as he has even begun begging for food (p. 24). The review is careful not to draw final conclusions, yet *contempt* is probably not too strong a word for its view of a radically simple missionary lifestyle:

> Self-imposed suffering is not of necessity sacrifice, and death, which is practically self-sought in a disregard of natural law and common human need, is more of suicide than of martyrdom. Besides, there is an asceticism of spirit, which shrinks from the self-indulgence of ostentatious outward peculiarity, but which is nobly efficacious in bracing the man to strongest efforts for the highest ends. For an Englishman to adopt a Hindu's dress and fare excites curiosity and comment, but whether it carries moral weight with it or not we question. (*The Harvest Field*, second series, vol. 5 no. 1, July 1884: 24)

The following month C. B. Ward is discussed again, this time because "in imitation apparently of the latest tactics of the Salvation Army" he began to dress like a Hindu sanyasi and went on a five-day tour without taking any food, depending on the local people to provide rations (p. 58). The concluding statement, a quote from the *Bombay Guardian*, is clear that this is considered a misguided affirmation of Hindu asceticism: "They wish to adorn the doctrine of Christ, but are really testifying to ideas that are much opposed to that doctrine" (*The Harvest Field*, second series, vol. 5 no. 2, Aug. 1884: 58).

A similar statement appeared in March of 1885, this time in a report from the Bangalore Missionary Conference.

> It was felt that while we honour the spirit which leads a man to give up European food, clothing, and manner of life, we cannot but regard such procedure as a distinct misrepresentation of Christianity, and as an unhappy homage to the ascetic spirit of Hinduism. (*The Harvest Field*, second series, vol. 5 no. 9, March 1885: 283)

This would have appeared just as Benjamin Robinson was beginning his first outreach from Gubbi that is described above in chapter 2.

But in April of 1885 various sides of the story come into clear view. W. H. Jackson Picken wrote an article in *The Harvest Field* in response to a paper published in *The Indian Evangelical Review,* in which J. G. Shome presented Christ and the apostles as faqirs[134] who lived exemplary lives of poverty that should be followed in India today. Picken reacts strongly against this and is decidedly opposed to "faqirism":

> Mr. Shome himself acknowledges that the word is not a happy one. We go further and say it would be nothing short of a libel on the inspired evangelists to suggest, that the sacred history of Christ and His apostles leaves us with the impression that they resembled in their mode of life those wretched, filth-loving beings who go about our Indian streets with ashes on their heads, clothed in their saffron-coloured garments and carrying a vessel in their hands, or a bag slung over their shoulders, for the reception of rice; while they mutter curses over those who refuse to give, or give too sparingly, and chant blessings over those who give with a liberal hand and a trembling heart. (Picken 1885, 296–97)

In bracketed editorial comments at the end of the article, *The Harvest Field* distanced itself from the strong stance Picken took:

> We do not suppose that the writer of the article in *The Indian Evangelical Review* wished that all missionaries should become preaching friars depending for their subsistence on the alms of the people. We ourselves are willing to admit that if "men of honest report full of the Holy Ghost and wisdom," feel themselves called to this work, and would go out *silently* as avant-couriers, they might do splendid service. (*The Harvest Field*, second series, vol. 5 no. 10, April 1885: 297; italics original)

Two years later, in May of 1887, *The Harvest Field* joined the chorus against the Salvation Army in a short piece under "Notes and Extracts" entitled "The Latest Freak of the Salvation Army." This refers to an Army scheme of wearing forehead markings: "A red mark is said to represent Christ's blood, a yellow one the fire of the Holy Ghost, and a blue one purity." *The Harvest Field* asks, "Cannot these good men see that these marks, instead of calling the people's attention to Christ and His religion only convince them that Christians are trying very hard to become Hindus?" (*The Harvest Field*, second series, vol. 7 no. 11, May 1887: 341).

---

134. The online Oxford dictionary says that a faqir is "a Muslim (or, loosely, a Hindu) religious ascetic who lives solely on alms" (https://en.oxforddictionaries.com/definition/fakir). Urdu and Hindi were only being defined (for political reasons) as separate Muslim (Urdu) and Hindu (Hindi) languages in the 1880s, so faqir when used in *The Harvest Field* in 1885 meant a renunciant (see Dalmia 2010, 169ff, on the creation of Hindi and Urdu in the late nineteenth century).

In June of 1887 *The Harvest Field* published a review of a Salvation Army report on 1886, including this comment on missionary lifestyles:

> We have not the slightest objection to the adoption of native garb. If the Army can do any good by it, then in the name of the Lord let them do it. What we object to is the tacit assumption of superiority over other missionaries which they base upon this. (*The Harvest Field*, second series, vol. 7 no. 12, June 1887: 355)

In May of 1888 the distinctive lifestyle of the Salvation Army in India is again brought up, and claims of success due to such measures are disputed.

> The only *specialities* about the Salvation Army are these—that its members denationalise themselves to the utmost possible extent and maintain themselves by begging. In no other respects do their methods differ essentially from those already pursued. They preach everywhere; so do others, with this advantage that they really know the language, and, in place of reciting a noisy and broken experience, are able to instruct clearly and consecutively. Of the importance of the specialities referred to the average missionary mind is not at all convinced…. And we affirm, with the utmost desire to learn wherever we can, that these peculiarities have so far impressed "the toiler in the rice fields" not one whit more than the talk of the man who dons a "*topi*" [hat] and wears boots. (*The Harvest Field*, second series, vol. 8 no. 11, May 1888: 381; italics original)

July of 1888 brought good news of changes of policy within the Salvation Army:

> We learn with satisfaction that the Salvation Army leaders are seeing the imprudence of their policy of poor food and unsuitable dress. Orders have been issued from head-quarters in London, that hereafter the girls may wear sun-hats, and have such food as their systems demand. The death rate and sick-rolls have properly modified the determination of the leaders to starve and be starved. We are delighted to learn, also, that General Booth has issued orders that henceforth the forehead marks are to be discontinued by the workers in South India. These things will greatly strengthen the probability of successful and permanent work in the country. (*The Harvest Field*, second series, vol. 9 no. 1, July 1888: 22)

But by October it seemed clear that nothing had changed. In a long, unsigned article entitled "The Salvation Army in India," there is lamentation over the damage done to workers by not providing properly for their food. Letters from Salvation Army workers (not letters of complaint, just of need) are shared, including some in broken health who were not given funds to return to England. Other criticisms related to evangelistic methods followed. This statement gives a good summary of the points related to the lifestyle question:

> We had hoped that a change for the better was impending, but that hope has been crushed by a recent letter in the *Indian War Cry* from Commissioner Tucker in which he says the officers must rely on their own exertions for support more than ever. This is greatly to be deplored, and such a policy will yet work out a terrible nemesis. The Army would lose nothing but gain much in the sympathies and support of the Christian world, by making healthy provision for its officers. (*The Harvest Field*, second series, vol. 9 no. 4, Oct. 1888: 141)

The long October article just quoted included information that a series of questions had been sent to the Army seeking clear information. The November 1888 issue contains both that letter and the reply sent by Commissioner Booth-Tucker. This discussion moves beyond the principles of missionary lifestyle to specifics of the Salvation Army, but in light of the negativity toward the Army in quotations above, it seems right to provide a small sampling of Booth-Tucker's lengthy defense:

> When I first commenced the life of a native it was confidently prophesied that I should not live for three months. Five years have now passed away, and I can assure you that I am at this moment in better health than when I commenced. I can speak with confidence, having tried personally both sides of the question, wearing the dress and eating the food of an ordinary Indian. Nor have I ever asked one of our officers to do what I have not cheerfully done myself. While, however, we feel the necessity of living as natives we fully realise the importance of watching over and caring for the health of our officers, and this I may say consumes not only a large amount of our time and attention, but also a considerable portion of our income....
>
> There is much more that I could say, but I refrain. The war requires me, and surely I have said enough to show that the successes of the past fully justify the measures that we have adopted. For the rest we can wait with boundless faith till the time when every criticism shall be silenced in the face of the millions of saved Indians who shall stand with us around the throne, and who will owe their salvation to the spirit of those who gladly filled up the measure of the sufferings of Christ, and counted not their own lives dear that the world might be the sooner saved. In prayer for you and your readers,

I am, Yours for the salvation of India at any cost,
Fakir Singh (F. de L. Booth-Tucker)
Commissioner, Salvation Army (*The Harvest Field*, second series, vol. 9 no. 5, Nov. 1888: 161, 164)

A lengthy editorial note follows, lamenting that few of the questions were answered in detail. Regarding the lifestyle question, this comment most clarifies the divide:

> The Commissioner still labours under the delusion that to dress like a native and eat like a native is to be very near to the native in spirit. But that is a *non sequitur,* as by this time he might well have discovered. If he prefers that method, so be it; but both length and efficiency of service will be secured by making better provision for the workers. (ibid., 165)

Booth-Tucker was not happy with these comments, and his letter saying that it is best for him to ignore the types of questions and criticisms that *The Harvest Field* was raising was published in January of 1889, with editorial comments lamenting this withdrawal and affirming that no hostility was present in the queries from *The Harvest Field*.

As part of a series of articles on various missions, the Salvation Army was featured in April of 1889. A long interview with Booth-Tucker was published, which included this series of lifestyle questions and answers:

> What principle has guided you in adopting native dress and habits?

> We want to get as near to the natives of India as possible, and we found our European modes of dress and habits were a barrier. We tried a modified form of dress, but that did not answer; so we went in wholly for the native mode of dress and living. My mode of putting on the lower cloth is really Singhalese. I adopted it, because having to mix with all classes it was thought more suitable, but as a rule our men officers (except in Ceylon) put their cloths on in purely Hindu fashion, and I often do so myself. We want to be uniform as well as Indian, and yet to have something that distinguishes us from all castes. For the same reason we shave our heads. By cutting his hair a native identifies himself with the English. By shaving we make ourselves more like natives, and show them that the acceptance of Christianity does not involve giving up any national custom.

But do you not think head-shaving is a mark of heathenism?

No. I regard it as a national mark, having no connection with caste, and as such we require all our men working among Hindus to observe it. I dare not put a stumbling block in the way of a man being saved, and I feel I should be doing so if by cutting my hair in European fashion I gave him the impression that in order to become a Christian he must do the same.

But what do you do among non-head-shaving castes?

We adapt ourselves to them. Head-shaving is compulsory only on those who work among Hindus. Those who work among Singhalese and Sikhs must wear their hair long and those who work among Muhammadans must cut their hair like them.

Have you discarded the wearing of marks on the forehead, and if so, why?

We do not forbid the wearing of marks, but practically it has been allowed to drop, chiefly because it was a good deal opposed by Christians and we felt the game was not worth the candle.

How does a purely vegetable diet suit your officers?

Better than a meat one. To the delicate and sick we allow meat if they require it. Personally I have better health now on a vegetable diet than I had when I ate meat. Our first difficulty was in knowing how to cook our food properly and make it palatable. This difficulty is now overcome. (*The Harvest Field*, second series, vol. 9 no. 10, April 1889: 333–34

A major analysis of the Salvation Army and their work in India was presented by Rev. W. Joss in the May 1889 edition of *The Harvest Field*. Joss briefly related the arrival in India and the stated aims of the Army, then began a long list of complaints against their work. His third point of complaint is "their violation of the true principle of adaptation." The biggest problem is an overemphasis on externals, and he goes on to discuss food, dress, the wearing of the sacred tuft of hair, and begging. This is all too lengthy to reproduce, but one statement shows a continuing adjustment being made by the Army:

> Permission has lately been given to those who desire it to wear a regulation shoe; but as an order has been issued that every one strong and weak must carry an umbrella, so there should be one that all *must* wear shoes, and for the same reason as is given in the former one, viz., that the strong should remember the weak and should set them an example. (Joss 1889, 371–72; italics original)

Joss ends his article with an impressive appeal to missionaries in India to reach out with assistance to Salvation Army workers whenever possible as they are good and sincere workers for the cause of Christ.

In August 1889 *The Harvest Field* published Benjamin Robinson's account of his experiment with Indian dress and Indian food, which includes his statement that "I could not shut my eyes to the fact that I had transgressed God's laws of health, and that six weeks' illness was a warning, as well as an indication as to true economy in God's service" (Robinson 1889b, 45). There is considerably less information on this topic in *The Harvest Field* in the succeeding months and years.

Since so much of this appendix is about the Salvation Army, it is fitting to close with a final piece about the Army, this from *The Harvest Field* in 1893. George W. Sawday wrote an analysis of the tenth annual report of the Salvation Army in India, stating in his introduction that "we are pleased to find there a growing appreciation of the difficulties of the work" (1893, 366). Sawday demonstrates this point from the report, then proceeds with some of the typical criticisms against the Army, mainly their exaggerated reporting of numbers and complaints against the extremes of simple lifestyle leading to unnecessary suffering.

The close of this article involves a claim that General Booth in Glasgow had made an extreme statement about the difficulty of work in India, and Sawday's hope for better times ahead:

> "I'll never send another officer to India. India has been the plague of my life. Nearly all my officers have broken down, or got married, or come home to get married." We only hope that the conversation has been correctly reported, and that brighter days are in store for the hardworking devoted soldiers of the Army. (ibid. 373)

This is immediately followed by editorial comments indicating that Booth denied making the quoted statement; Booth suggested that health failures in the Salvation Army in India were not worse than in other mission societies. Nonetheless, Booth also affirmed that European officers would not be sent to India again in the large numbers that had been sent earlier.

References

App, Urs. 2010. *The Birth of Orientalism*. Philadelphia: University of Pennsylvania Press.

Basham, A. L. 2004 [1954]. *The Wonder that Was India: A Survey of the History and Culture of the Indian Subcontinent before the Coming of the Muslims*. Third Revised Edition. London: Picador.

Boyd, Robin H. S. 1974. *India and the Latin Captivity of the Church: The Cultural Context of the Gospel*. London: Cambridge University Press.

Browning, Robert. 1895. *The Complete Poetic and Dramatic Works of Robert Browning*. Cambridge Edition. Boston: Houghton, Mifflin and Company.

Cotton, James Sutherland, Richard Burn, and William Stevenson Meyer. 1908. *The Imperial Gazetteer of India, Vol. 18: Moram to Nayāgarh*. Oxford: The Clarendon Press.

Cox, Jeffrey. 2002. *Imperial Fault Lines: Christianity and Colonial Power in India, 1838–1940*. Stanford: Stanford University Press.

Dalmia, Vasudha. 2010 [1997]. *The Nationalization of Hindu Traditions: Bharatendu Harishchandra and Nineteenth-Century Banaras*. Reprinted with a new foreword by Francesca Orsini. Ranikhet: Permanent Black.

De Bary, Wm. Theodore, ed. 1958. *Sources of Indian Tradition*. Two volumes. New York: Columbia University Press.

Devadoss, D. 1946. *Life of Poet H. A. Krishna Pillai*. Madras: N.M.S. Press.

Dubois, Abbé J. A. 1995 [1823]. *Letters on the State of Christianity in India, to Which is Added a Vindication of the Hindus, Male and Female*. New Delhi: Asian Educational Services.

Dubois, Abbé J. A., and Henry K. Beauchamp. 1906. *Hindu Manners, Customs and Ceremonies*. Oxford: Clarendon Press.

Emilsen, William W. 1994. *Violence and Atonement: The Missionary Experiences of Mohandas Gandhi, Samuel Stokes and Verrier Elwin in India before 1935*. Studies in the Intercultural History of Christianity. Frankfurt: Peter Lang.

Farquhar, J. N. 1915. *The Crown of Hinduism*. London: Oxford University Press.

Findlay, G. G., and W. W. Holdsworth. 1921. *The History of the Wesleyan Methodist Missionary Society*. Vol. 1. London: The Epworth Press.

———. 1924. *The History of the Wesleyan Methodist Missionary Society.* Vol. 5. London: The Epworth Press.

Gleanings. 1883. "Gleanings." *The Harvest Field*, second series, vol. 3 no. 11, March 1883: 347–50. (Online at http://findit.library.yale.edu/catalog/digcoll:182778.)

Goel, Sita Ram. 2009. *Catholic Ashrams, Sannyasins or Swindlers?* Enlarged edition with new appendices. New Delhi: Voice of Truth.

Haigh, Henry. 1893. "Vernacular Literature." In *Report of the Third Decennial Missionary Conference held at Bombay, 1892–93, Vol. 2*, edited by A. Mainwaring, 664–74. Bombay: Education Society's Steam Press.

Hedlund, Roger. 1995. "Post Missionary Asia: One Size Doesn't Fit All." *Evangelical Missions Quarterly* vol. 31 no. 1, Jan. 1995: 78–84.

Hutton, J. H. 1961. *Caste in India: Its Nature, Function, and Origins.* Third edition. London: Oxford University Press.

Inden, Ronald. 1990. *Imagining India.* Cambridge, MA: Blackwell.

Joss, W. 1889. "The Salvation Army in India." *The Harvest Field*, second series, vol. 9 no. 11, May 1889: 368–81. (Online at http://findit.library.yale.edu/catalog/digcoll:182850.)

Kent, Eliza F. 2009. "'What's Written on the Forehead Will Never Fail': Karma, Fate, and Headwriting in Indian Folktales." *Asian Ethnology* vol. 68 no. 1: 1–16.

King, Richard. 1991. *Orientalism and Religion: Postcolonial Theory, India and "The Mystic East."* New Delhi: Oxford University Press.

Klostermaier, Klaus K. 1994. *A Survey of Hinduism.* Second edition. Albany, NY: State University of New York Press.

Krishnananda, Swami. 1977. *The Māndūkya Upaniṣad: An Exposition.* Shivanandanagar: The Divine Life Society.

McKenzie, John. 1929. "Higher Education." In *The Christian Task in India*, edited by John McKenzie, 85–102. London: Macmillan and Co.

Methodist Publishing House. 1912. *An Alphabetical and Chronological Arrangement of the Wesleyan Methodist Ministers and Preachers on Trial in the British and Irish Conferences.* 22nd edition. London: The Methodist Publishing House.

Murr, Sylvia. 1987. *L'Inde philosophique entre Bossuet et Voltaire.* Paris: Ecole francaise d'Extreme-Orient.

Mysore. 1889. "The Month's Mission News, Wesleyan: The Mysore District." *The Harvest Field*, third series, vol. 1 no. 4, Oct. 1889: 141. (Online at http://findit.library.yale.edu/catalog/digcoll:182855.)

Notes. 1889. "Editorial Notes." *The Harvest Field*, third series, vol. 1 no. 3, Sept. 1889: 119–20. (Online at http://findit.library.yale.edu/catalog/digcoll:182854.)

Oddie, Geoffrey. 2006. *Imagined Hinduism: British Protestant Missionary Constructions of Hinduism, 1793–1900.* New Delhi: Sage Publications.

Olivelle, Patrick. 2006. *Manu's Code of Law: A Critical Edition and Translation of the* Mānava Dharmaśāstra. New Delhi: Oxford University Press.

Personalia. 1889. "Chronicle of the Stations: Personalia." *The Harvest Field,* second series, vol. 9 no. 7, Jan. 1889: 241. (Online at http://findit.library.yale.edu/catalog/digcoll:182846.)

Picken, W. H. Jackson. 1885. "Fakirism as a Mode of Evangelistic Work." *The Harvest Field*, second series, vol. 5 no. 10, April 1885: 289–97. (Online at http://findit.library.yale.edu/catalog/digcoll:182801.)

Quigley, Declan. 1994. "Is a Theory of Caste Still Possible?" In *Contextualising Caste*, edited by Ursula Sharma and Mary Searle-Chatterjee, 25–48. Oxford: Blackwell.

Robinson, Benjamin. 1885a (anonymous). "Memories I." *The Harvest Field,* second series, vol. 6 no. 1, July 1885: 5–10. (Online at http://findit.library.yale.edu/catalog/digcoll:182804.)

———. 1885b (anonymous). "Memories II." *The Harvest Field*, second series, vol. 6 no. 2, Aug. 1885: 43–49. (Online at http://findit.library.yale.edu/catalog/digcoll:182805.)

———. 1885c (anonymous). "Memories III." *The Harvest Field*, second series, vol. 6 no. 3, Sept. 1885: 76–83. (Online at http://findit.library.yale.edu/catalog/digcoll:182806.)

———. 1885d (anonymous, almost surely by Robinson). "My Munshi." *The Harvest Field,* second series, vol. 6 no. 4, Oct. 1885: 103–6. (Online at http://findit.library.yale.edu/catalog/digcoll:182807.)

———. 1885e (A. Vidyarthi ["a student"]). "Among the Hindu Villagers." *The Harvest Field*, second series, vol. 6 no. 5, Nov. 1885: 139–46. (Online at http://findit.library.yale.edu/catalog/digcoll:182808.)

———. 1889a (anonymous). "An Experiment in Mission Work I." *The Harvest Field*, second series, vol. 9 no. 11, May 1889: 361–65. (Online at http://findit.library.yale.edu/catalog/digcoll:182850.)

———. 1889b. "An Experiment in Mission Work II." *The Harvest Field*, third series, vol. 1 no. 2, Aug. 1889: 41–45. (Online at http://findit.library.yale.edu/catalog/digcoll:182853.)

Sargent, N. C. 1939. "Indian Dress: The Story of a Costly Experiment." *National Christian Council Review*, vol. 59 no. 2, Feb. 1939: 85–89.

Sawday, G. W. 1885. "Hinduism: Past and Present, Second Paper." *The Harvest Field*, second series, vol. 5 no. 11, May 1885: 321–28. (Online at http://findit.library.yale.edu/catalog/digcoll:182802.)

———. 1893. "The Salvation Army in India." *The Harvest Field*, third series, vol. 4 no. 10, April 1893: 366–73. (Online at http://findit.library.yale.edu/catalog/digcoll:182897.)

Schouten, J. P. 1995. *Revolution of the Mystics: On the Social Aspects of Vīraśaivism.* Delhi: Motilal Banarsidass.

Shah, A. M. 2006. "Sects and Hindu Social Structure." *Contributions to Indian Sociology,* vol. 40 no. 2, June 2006: 209–48.

Sharma, Arvind. 2003. "Introduction." In *The Study of Hinduism. Studies in Comparative Religion*, edited by Arvind Sharma, ix–xii. Columbia, SC: University of South Carolina Press.

———. 2017. *The Ruler's Gaze: A Study of British Rule over India from a Saidian Perspective.* Noida: HarperCollins.

Singh, K. S. 1992. *People of India: An Introduction.* National Series Vol. One: The People of India. Calcutta: Anthropological Survey of India.

———. 2003. *People of India: Karnataka.* Vol. 26, part one. New Delhi: Affiliated East-West Press.

Stone, Anthony Philip. 1981. *Hindu Astrology: Myths, Symbols and Realities.* New Delhi: Select Books.

van Buitenen, J. A. B. 1973. *The Mahābhārata, 1. The Book of the Beginning.* Two volumes. Chicago: University of Chicago Press.

———. 1975. *The Mahābhārata, 2. The Book of the Assembly Hall, 3. The Book of the Forest.* Chicago: University of Chicago Press.

Walker, Benjamin. 1983. *Hindu World: An Encyclopedic Survey of Hinduism.* Two volumes. New Delhi: Munshiram Manoharlal.

Wesleyan. 1889. "The Month's Mission News, Wesleyan: Another Break-down in Mysore." *The Harvest Field*, third series, vol. 1 no. 5, Nov. 1889: 192. (Online at http://findit.library.yale.edu/catalog/digcoll:182856.)

Wesleyan Methodist Church. 1800s. *The Catechisms of the Wesleyan Methodists.* London: Wesleyan Methodist Book Room.

———. 1913. *Minutes of Several Conversations at the One Hundred and Seventieth Yearly Conference of the People Called Methodists in the Connexion Established by the Late Rev. John Wesley, a.m., begun in Plymouth on Wednesday, July 16, 1913.* London: Wesleyan Conference Office.

Wesleyan Methodist News. 1885. "Wesleyan Methodist News: Bangalore Missionary Conference." *The Harvest Field*, second series, vol. 5 no. 9, March 1885: 282–83. (Online at http://findit.library.yale.edu/catalog/digcoll:182800.)

Winternitz, M. 1985. *History of Indian Literature, Vol. III Part I: Classical Sanskrit Literature.* Delhi: Motilal Banarsidass.

INDEX

A

advaita philosophy 4, 41, 42
Anglo-Mysore wars xix
asceticism/austerity in mission xii, xxi, xxviii, 70, 77

B

bhakti (devotion) xxiv, xxvii-xxviii, 2, 38, 41, 59
Bhagavad Gita 1, 2
Booth, William 75, 76, 79, 83
Booth-Tucker, Frederick see *Tucker*
Boyd, Robin xxiii
Brāhmans xxvii, 3, 4–5, 8, 14, 15, 25, 29–31, 33, 35–43, 46–52, 58
British imperialism xxxiii, 6–7, 15, 38–39, 48
Britten, I. see *Robinson, Benjamin wife*
Buddha/ism 18–19, 37, 42

C

caste xxii, xxiv, xxv-xxvi, xxix, 2–5, 14, 17, 24–28, 33, 46–47, 50, 52, 57–58, 61, 66, 81–82
Chetti, Kandiswamy 63
Christianity xvii, xviii, xxi-xxv, xxix, 7, 36, 61–63, 65, 77, 81–82
   denominationalism 36, 62
   failure in India/Asia xvii, xviii, xix, xxv, 9–10, 36, 62
   foreign religion xxii-xxiii, xxiv, xxv, xxix, 25, 48, 61, 65, 81–82
   contextualization xii, xiii, xx, xxv, xxxiii, 11–21, 25, 27, 28, 37, 46, 48, 61–62, 81–82
   contextual theology xxiii, xxiv, xxviii, xxix, 42
converts to Christianity xxiv, 46–48
culture xi, xii, xviii, xxii, xxvi, xxix, 5, 12–15, 62
culture gaps xii, xiii, xvii, xxii, xxxiii–xxxiv, 5–6, 7, 10, 17, 28, 65

D

dalits xvii, 5, 19, 46, 52, 58
de Nobili, Roberto xxii
devotion see *bhakti*
dharma 2, 5, 19, 26, 35, 59
Dubois, Abbe xxiii, 9

E

educational missions xix, xxi, xxviii, 14, 16, 25, 34, 39, 46, 52–53
evangelism xiii, xvii-xviii, xxiii-xxiv, 15, 20, 28–29, 35, 37, 43, 46, 49, 53, 57–58, 62

F

Farquhar, J. N. xxv, 63
fulfillment theology xxv, 63

G

Gersoppa Falls 6

H

Haigh, Henry xxix, xxxiii-xxxiv, 61
Harvest Field, The xx, 65, 76
Hindu followers of Jesus xviii, 16, 25, 39, 48, 61–63
Hindus/Hinduism xxv, xxvi-xxviii, 3–6, 27, 29, 33, 36, 37, 38, 43, 62, 66
Hoysala kingdom xix
Hyder Ali xix

I

insider movements xviii

International Review of Missions xviii, 65

interreligious engagement xviii, xxiii, xxv, 6, 9, 16, 19–20, 35–36, 48–52, 61–63

J

Jains 8, 18, 19

L

Lingāyats xxvii, 3, 6, 7, 8, 16, 42

M

Mādhvas xxvii-xxviii, 4, 48–50

Mark, John 11–21

missionary lifestyle controversy xii, xix, xx, xxi-xxii, xxxi, 27–28, 55, 75–83

missionary limitations xii, xvii-xviii, 6, 20, 57, 63, 83

missionary need to learn xxiii, see also Robinson, Benjamin, learning always

multiple religious belonging xviii

N

non-baptized believers in Christ see Hindu followers of Jesus

O

Orientalism xxxv-xxvi, xxxiii

P

parables from Indian life 1, 24, 26,

Parasurāma 33, 40

proverbs, Indian 21, 26, 35, 58

R

Rāma 41

Ramanuja xxvii, xxviii

Roberts, Julia 3

Robinson, Benjamin
  betrothal xx, 69–74
  birth xx
  local clothing and diet xii, xiii, xxii, xxviii, 7, 8–10, 11–15, 20, 23, 25–27, 46, 55, 57, 62, 69
  death xii, xxi
  early commitment to India xx
  encounters with Hindus 3, 4, 6, 7, 8, 14, 16, 18, 19–20, 29–30, 38–39, 41, 48–52
  health problems xii, xviii, xix, xx, xxii, xxviii, 21, 23, 27, 43, 53, 55–57, 69, 71
  humility xvii-xviii, xx, xxiv, 7, 10, 25, 28–29, 37–38, 63
  learning always xii, xvii, xix, xx, xxx, xxxiii, 17, 28–29, 30–31, 34, 35, 37, 64
  language study xxx, xxxi, xxxiii, 30–31, 34, 57, 70
  marriage xx, 70–71, 74
  ministry in UK xx, xxi, 57
  missionary opposition to xi, xviii, xxi, xxii, xxxi, 24
  regrets at his departure from India xix, 56
  undeveloped potential xix, xxiv, 62–63
  wife I. Britten xxviii, 55–57, 74
  writings xxx, 87
  zeal xx, xxviii, xxxiii, 6, 10, 20, 37, 52, 57, 69

S

Salvation Army xxi, 48, 75-83

Sankara (Sankaracharya) 29, 41, 42

Sanskrit xix, xxx, 5, 19, 26, 30, 31, 34–35, 38, 41, 48, 50, 53, 58

Shakuntalā 35

Smārtas 4, 29, 42, 48, 50

Srivaishnavas xxvii, 4, 38

T

Tipu Sultan xix

Titus, Daya Prakash 61

Tucker, Frederick 76–77, 80–81

U

Upanishads 2, 40, 42, 58

V

Vedas xxvii, 2, 3, 15, 30, 40, 42–43, 49–51, 58

W

Wesleyan Methodist Missionary Society xix, 9, 10, 75

www.ingramcontent.com/pod-product-compliance
Ingram Content Group UK Ltd.
Pitfield, Milton Keynes, MK11 3LW, UK
UKHW022240230426
12048UKWH00018BA/1372